MEDITERRANEAN DIET
beginners cookbook

Dr. Lavinia Baresi

Dear Reader,

Thank you for purchasing my book and supporting the two things I love: researching recipes and sharing healthy cooking with others.

Usually, this happens in our kitchen over a glass of wine with friends and family, filled with silly jokes. Today, I'm fortunate to share some of these moments with you in my book.

If you have just 20 seconds, please rate my book on Amazon. Your honest review would mean the world to my publishing venture, to me, and to my family! I promise to pay this kindness forward in other moments of my life.

Here is a QR code to make it super easy.

Thank you!

Lavinia

Just one last thing...

I'm giving away **10 of my favorite, handpicked recipes** from the next book (complete with color photos of the dishes) **for free**, no strings attached!

If you're interested, please follow this QR link:

FOREWORD

As I sit with pen in hand, eager to share my culinary journey, memories of my childhood along the sun-drenched shores of Santa Margherita flood my mind. The salty sea breeze and the fragrance of lemon blossoms define my early years in this picturesque Ligurian town, where the azure Mediterranean waves kissed rugged cliffs and ancient olive groves. I am **Lavinia Baresi**, and I invite you into my world.

Raised in a family deeply rooted in the Mediterranean lifestyle, my Nonna and Nonno taught me the art of living well. We spent countless hours in the local markets, engaging in a ritual that connected us to the earth and sea, choosing vegetables, fruits, meats, and fish that were not just food but a celebration of nature's abundance.

From the earliest days, the rich aromas of ripe tomatoes, fragrant basil, and robust olive oil filled our home, setting the stage for a life where food transcended mere sustenance. It was about stories and traditions, an ongoing dialogue with generations past.

One of my fondest childhood memories is of fishing with my Nonno. Together, we'd set out in his modest boat, armed with a large towel and bait, aiming to snare tiny shrimps from the warm, shallow waters. We caught a needlefish on a particularly unforgettable day instead of the usual shrimps. Its long, sleek body glistened with a silver sheen, dazzling my young eyes as I held it. Later that evening, we cooked our day's haul, shrimps included, in a big pan over an open fire in our garden. As we did, the ground around us sparkled, lit by plankton that the sea had brought to shore, casting a magical glow that danced under the stars.

My passion for understanding the intricate relationship between diet and wellness grew as I matured, ultimately shaping my career. I delved deeply into the Mediterranean diet, which is far more than a dietary plan—it's a holistic approach to life. Emphasizing balance and moderation, it enriches every meal with the joy of flavors that range from subtle to bold, all while fostering community and connection.

Life gifted me another treasure—my wonderful American husband, who also marked a pivotal moment in my career as a nutritionist and dietician. I quickly noticed his distinct approach to food, which differed significantly from mine. Gradually, I've steered him toward a more thoughtful and enriching relationship with food. He wholeheartedly embraced the Mediterranean diet, known for its benefits in promoting longevity and overall health, and has been my inspiration and support in writing this book.

Join me as we celebrate the Mediterranean way, from the vibrant landscapes of Greece to the diverse coasts of Northern Africa. In this world, each meal is an occasion brimming with life, love, and happiness.

This book is a heartfelt tribute to anyone new to the Mediterranean diet or seeking to deepen their understanding. Here, you will find simple, nourishing recipes that embody the region's spirit—dishes that feed the body and soothe the soul. Together, let's embark on this flavorful voyage.

BASICS OF MEDITERRANEAN DIET

UNDERSTANDING THE MEDITERRANEAN DIET

The Mediterranean diet, known as the Med diet, is often heralded as the gold eating standard, praised for its health benefits and longevity-promoting properties. It encompasses foods common in countries surrounding the Mediterranean Sea, focusing on whole grains, fruits, vegetables, fish, nuts, and olive oil. Red meat and sweets are consumed in moderation to avoid high intakes of saturated fats and added sugars.

STARTING YOUR MEDITERRANEAN JOURNEY

Embarking on the Mediterranean diet begins with simple, accessible changes. Replace processed foods with whole foods, add vegetables as side dishes, and swap sugary drinks for fresh fruit or herbal tea. Gradually incorporate Mediterranean dishes like hummus or lentils to familiarize yourself with the flavors.

ESSENTIAL FOODS TO EMBRACE

The Mediterranean diet is a lifestyle, not a restrictive meal plan. It encourages a wide range of whole foods, focusing on protein intake. Essential foods include seafood like salmon and sardines, rich in omega-3 fatty acids, legumes like chickpeas and lentils, and a variety of fruits and vegetables that provide antioxidants, vitamins, and fibre.

FOODS TO LIMIT

To maximize health benefits, avoid processed, sugary foods and unhealthy fats. Limit fried foods and processed meats. The goal isn't to eliminate food groups and consciously limit unhealthy choices. Moderate red meat, dairy, and refined carbs are acceptable, with balance essential.

LIFESTYLE CHANGES AND BENEFITS

The Mediterranean diet also emphasizes lifestyle changes. Regular physical activity and moderate alcohol intake, such as red wine, known for its antioxidants, promote weight loss, reduce the risk of heart disease, and may extend life expectancy.

THE SCIENCE BEHIND THE MEDITERRANEAN DIET

Research highlights the profound impact of the Mediterranean diet on longevity and health. A Norwegian study published in PLOS Medicine found that adopting the Mediterranean diet can significantly extend lifespan. This diet is rich in antioxidants, phytochemicals, omega-3 fatty acids, and fibre, which work synergistically to improve health and reduce disease risk.

KEY HEALTH BENEFITS

1. Reduces Risk of Heart Disease and Stroke: Research indicates that adherence to the Mediterranean diet significantly reduces the risk of heart attack, stroke, and coronary artery disease.

2. Minimizes Effects of Stress and Quells Inflammation: The diet appears to counteract stress-related inflammation, reducing cortisol levels and inflammatory markers.

3. Lowers Cancer Risk and Recurrence: High levels of antioxidants and anti-inflammatory compounds in the diet protect against cancer and reduce the risk of recurrence and mortality.

4. Decreases Risk of Type 2 Diabetes and Complications: The Mediterranean diet lowers the risk of developing type 2 diabetes and reduces complications for those diagnosed with the condition.

5. Slows Cognitive Decline: Adherence to the diet slows age-related memory loss and cognitive decline, benefiting those with and without dementia.

6. Promotes Bone Density: The diet helps prevent fragility by minimizing bone and muscle loss associated with ageing.

CONTENT

BREAKFAST — 06 13

FISH & SEAFOOD — 14 21

MEAT — 22 30

PASTA — 31 38

POULTRY — 39 46

PULSES — 47 54

SALADS & MEZZES — 55 63

SOUP — 64 72

SPICES & SAUCES — 73 82

VEGETARIAN	83	91
MOCKTAILS	92	97
MEDITERRANEAN DIET PYRAMID	98	
CONVERSION TABLE	99	
MEAL PLAN. SHOPPING LIST	100	107
INDEX PAGE	108	110

BREAKFAST

BREAKFAST

EGG WHITE SCRAMBLE WITH ASPARAGUS AND SUN-DRIED TOMATOES, ITALY

INGREDIENTS

- 6 large egg whites (about 7 oz or 198g)
- 1/2 cup chopped asparagus tips (about 2.4 oz or 67g)
- 1/4 cup chopped sun-dried tomatoes (about 1 oz or 28g)
- 1/4 cup finely diced onions (about 1.4 oz or 40g)
- 1 tablespoon olive oil (0.5 fl oz or 15ml)
- 1/4 teaspoon salt (0.05 oz or 1.5g)
- 1/4 teaspoon black pepper (0.02 oz or 0.5g)
- 1/4 cup crumbled feta cheese (optional) (about 1 oz or 30g)
- 1 tablespoon chopped fresh basil (0.1 oz or 3g)

METHOD PAN | **TIME** 20 MINUTE | **SERVING** 2 PERSON | **CALORIES** 150

Awaken your taste buds with this splendid breakfast creation that's as nourishing as it is flavorful. This dish pairs fluffy egg whites with the vibrant snap of fresh asparagus and the deep, sweet tang of sun-dried tomatoes, crafting a morning meal that's both healthful and delightfully satisfying. Perfect for those who crave a light yet protein-rich start to their day.

- ✓ Non-stick skill
- ✓ Mixing bowl
- ✓ Cutting board
- ✓ Knife
- ✓ Whisk

INSTRUCTIONS

Step 1 | Heat the olive oil
Heat the olive oil (0.5 fl oz or 15ml) in a non-stick skillet over medium heat.

Step 2 | Sauté Onions and Asparagus
Add the onions (1.4 oz or 40g) and asparagus tips (2.4 oz or 67g) to the skillet, sautéing until the onions are translucent and the asparagus is tender-crisp, about 3-4 minutes.

Step 3 | Add Sun-Dried Tomatoes
Stir in the chopped sun-dried tomatoes (1 oz or 28g) and cook for another minute, allowing the flavors to meld.

Step 4 | Whisk Egg Whites
In a bowl, whisk together the egg whites (7 oz or 198g), salt (0.05 oz or 1.5g), and pepper (0.02 oz or 0.5g) until frothy.

Step 5 | Cook Egg Whites
Pour the frothy egg whites over the sautéed vegetables in the skillet, stirring gently to combine. Allow the egg whites to set on the bottom for about a minute, then gently stir the mixture, cooking until the egg whites are fully set but still moist, approximately 3-5 minutes.

Step 6 | Add Feta (Optional)
If using feta cheese (1 oz or 30g), sprinkle it over the scramble just before it's fully cooked.

Step 7 | Garnish and Serve
Once cooked, remove from heat and garnish with fresh basil (0.1 oz or 3g). Serve immediately and enjoy this vibrant Mediterranean-inspired dish.

NOTES

- For a complete Mediterranean breakfast, pair this egg white scramble with whole-grain toast and a side of mixed greens drizzled with olive oil and lemon juice.

- This dish is not only low in calories and fat but also rich in high-quality protein, vitamins, and antioxidants thanks to the asparagus and sun-dried tomatoes.

BREAKFAST

2 ROASTED RED PEPPER AND FETA FRITTATA, CYPRUS

Experience the bold and delightful flavors of the Mediterranean with our Roasted Red Pepper and Feta Frittata. This dish blends the smoky sweetness of roasted red peppers with the creamy tang of feta cheese, creating a mouth-watering and nutritious meal that's perfect for any time of day.

METHOD OVEN | **TIME** 30 MINUTE | **SERVING** 4 PERSON | **CALORIES** 320

- ✓ Oven
- ✓ 10-inch ovenproof skillet
- ✓ Cutting board
- ✓ Knife
- ✓ Mixing bowl
- ✓ Whisk

INGREDIENTS

- 6 large eggs (about 12 oz or 340g)
- 1/2 cup whole milk (4 fl oz or 120ml)
- 1 cup diced roasted red peppers (about 5.3 oz or 150g)
- 3/4 cup crumbled feta cheese (about 3.5 oz or 100g)
- 1/4 cup chopped fresh basil leaves (about 0.9 oz or 25g)
- 2 tablespoons olive oil (1 fl oz or 30ml)
- 1/2 teaspoon salt (0.09 oz or 2.5g)
- 1/4 teaspoon black pepper (0.02 oz or 0.5g)
- 1/4 teaspoon red pepper flakes (optional) (0.02 oz or 0.5g)

NOTES

- This frittata is equally delicious served hot or at room temperature, making it a versatile option for meals or quick snacks.
- Leftovers keep well in the refrigerator for up to 2 days, ensuring a ready-to-eat, healthy option is always on hand.

INSTRUCTIONS

Step 1 | Preheat Oven
Preheat your oven to 375°F (190°C).

Step 2 | Mix Eggs and Milk
In a mixing bowl, whisk together the eggs (12 oz or 340g), milk (4 fl oz or 120ml), salt (0.09 oz or 2.5g), black pepper (0.02 oz or 0.5g), and red pepper flakes (0.02 oz or 0.5g) if using, until well combined.

Step 3 | Sauté Peppers
Heat the olive oil (1 fl oz or 30ml) in a 10-inch ovenproof skillet over medium heat. Add the diced roasted red peppers (5.3 oz or 150g) and sauté for 2 minutes until they are heated through.

Step 4 | Add Egg Mixture
Pour the egg mixture into the skillet over the roasted red peppers, ensuring the peppers are evenly distributed.

Step 5 | Add Feta and Basil
Sprinkle the crumbled feta cheese (3.5 oz or 100g) and chopped basil (0.9 oz or 25g) evenly over the top of the egg mixture.

Step 6 | Cook on Stovetop
Cook on the stovetop for about 5 minutes until the edges begin to set.

Step 7 | Bake
Transfer the skillet to the preheated oven and bake for 20 minutes, or until the frittata is set and the top is lightly golden.

Step 8 | Serve
Remove from the oven and let it sit for a couple of minutes. Then, slice the frittata into wedges and serve.

BREAKFAST

3 OVERNIGHT OATS WITH GREEK YOGURT AND FRESH FIGS, GREECE

METHOD — MIXING
TIME — 10 MINUTE
SERVING — 2 PERSON
CALORIES — 350

Start your day with the enchanting flavors of Overnight Oats with Greek Yogurt and Fresh Figs. This sublime mix marries the lush creaminess of Greek yogurt with the honeyed allure of ripe figs for a breakfast that's both effortlessly prepared and wholesomely satisfying.

- Medium-sized mixing bowl
- Measuring cups and spoons
- Spoon for mixing
- Serving bowls or jars

INGREDIENTS

- 1 cup rolled oats (about 3.2 oz or 90g)
- 1 cup unsweetened almond milk (about 4.2 oz or 120g)
- 1/2 cup Greek yogurt (about 4.2 oz or 120g)
- 2 tablespoons honey (about 1.05 fl oz or 30ml), **plus extra for drizzling**
- 1/2 teaspoon vanilla extract (about 0.085 fl oz or 2.5ml)
- 1/4 teaspoon ground cinnamon (about 0.02 oz or 0.5g)
- Pinch of salt
- 4 fresh figs, quartered (about 5.6 oz or 160g)
- Optional toppings: chopped nuts, seeds, additional Greek yogurt

NOTES

- The oats can be prepared up to 2 days in advance and stored in the refrigerator.
- Feel free to customize the recipe with your favorite fruits or toppings.
- Use gluten-free oats for a gluten-free version of this recipe.

INSTRUCTIONS

Step 1 | Combine Oats and Milk
In a medium-sized mixing bowl, combine the rolled oats (3.2 oz or 90g) and unsweetened almond milk (8.5 fl oz or 240ml). Stir until the oats are fully immersed in the liquid.

Step 2 | Add Yogurt and Flavorings
Add Greek yogurt (4.2 oz or 120g) to the oat mixture, drizzling in the honey (1.05 fl oz or 30ml), vanilla extract (0.085 fl oz or 2.5ml), ground cinnamon (0.02 oz or 0.5g), and a pinch of salt. Mix thoroughly to ensure all ingredients are well incorporated.

Step 3 | Refrigerate
Cover the bowl with a lid or plastic wrap and place it in the refrigerator overnight, or for at least 8 hours, to allow the oats to absorb the liquid and flavors to meld.

Step 4 | Adjust Consistency
The next morning, give the oats a good stir. If the mixture is too thick, you can thin it out with a little more almond milk to reach your desired consistency.

Step 5 | Serve
Divide the oat mixture between two serving bowls or jars. Top each serving with fresh quartered figs (5.6 oz or 160g), adding a drizzle of honey for extra sweetness if desired. For added texture and nutrients, sprinkle with optional toppings like chopped nuts or seeds. Serve immediately or keep refrigerated until ready to eat.

BREAKFAST

4 SPANISH CHORIZO SHAKSHUKA WITH PIQUILLO PEPPERS, SPAIN

INGREDIENTS

- 1 tablespoon olive oil (0.5 fl oz or 15ml)
- 4 ounces Spanish chorizo, sliced (about 4 oz or 113g)
- 1 medium onion, diced (about 1 cup or 150g)
- 2 cloves garlic, minced (about 0.35 oz or 10g)
- 1 teaspoon smoked paprika (about 0.11 oz or 3g)
- 1/2 teaspoon cumin (about 0.05 oz or 1.5g)
- 1/4 teaspoon cayenne pepper (optional) (about 0.025 oz or 0.75g)
- 1 can crushed tomatoes (14 oz or 400g)
- 1 jar piquillo peppers, sliced (7 oz or 198g)
- 4 large eggs
- Salt and pepper, to taste
- Fresh parsley, chopped for garnish
- Crusty bread, for serving

METHOD PAN
TIME 15 MINUTE
SERVING 4 PERSON
CALORIES 320

Savor the essence of Spanish cuisine with the Spanish Chorizo Shakshuka, featuring fiery chorizo and sweet piquillo peppers nestled among gently poached eggs. This robust and colorful dish promises a delightful culinary adventure, perfect for a spirited breakfast or brunch.

- ✓ Large, deep skillet
- ✓ Cutting board
- ✓ Chef's knife
- ✓ Can opener
- ✓ Spoon for stirring and making wells
- ✓ Measuring spoons
- ✓ Lid for the skillet

INSTRUCTIONS

Step 1 | Prepare the Chorizo
Heat the olive oil (0.5 fl oz or 15ml) in a large, deep skillet over medium heat. Add the sliced chorizo (4 oz or 113g) and cook until it starts to brown and release its oils, about 3-4 minutes.

Step 2 | Sauté the Vegetables
Add the diced onion (1 cup or 150g) to the skillet with the chorizo and sauté until the onion is soft and translucent, about 5 minutes. Stir in the minced garlic (0.35 oz or 10g) and cook for another minute until fragrant.

Step 3 | Season the Base
Sprinkle in the smoked paprika (0.11 oz or 3g), cumin (0.05 oz or 1.5g), and cayenne pepper (0.025 oz or 0.75g). Stir the spices into the mixture and cook for about 1 minute to release their flavors.

Step 4 | Add Tomatoes and Peppers
Pour in the crushed tomatoes (14 oz or 400g) and add the sliced piquillo peppers (7 oz or 198g). Season with salt and pepper to taste. Let the mixture simmer for 10 minutes, stirring occasionally, until it thickens slightly.

Step 5 | Poach the Eggs
Make four wells in the sauce with a spoon. Crack an egg into each well. Cover the skillet with a lid and cook for 5-7 minutes, or until the eggs are cooked to your desired level of doneness.

Step 6 | Garnish and Serve
Remove the skillet from the heat. Garnish the shakshuka with chopped fresh parsley. Serve hot with crusty bread for dipping into the sauce and egg yolks.

NOTES

- For a vegetarian version, omit the chorizo and add extra smoked paprika for flavor.
- Adjust the heat level by increasing or decreasing the amount of cayenne pepper.
- Ensure your eggs are fresh for the best poaching results.
- If piquillo peppers are unavailable, roasted red peppers make a good substitute.
- Serve as part of a larger brunch spread or enjoy as a flavorful start to your day.

BREAKFAST

5 SAVORY OATMEAL WITH SPINACH AND POACHED EGGS, FRANCE

The comforting texture of oatmeal meets the sumptuous layers of sautéed spinach topped with perfectly poached eggs. This nourishing dish is a delightful twist on classic breakfast fare, offering a wholesome and satisfying meal to energize your day or wind down your evening.

METHOD PAN | **TIME** 20 MINUTE | **SERVING** 2 PERSON | **CALORIES** 350

- Small pot for poaching eggs
- Medium saucepan
- Slotted spoon
- Measuring cups and spoons

INGREDIENTS

- 1 cup rolled oats (about 3.2 oz or 90g)
- 2 cups water or low-sodium vegetable broth (16 fl oz or 480ml)
- 1/2 tsp extra virgin olive oil (about 0.085 fl oz or 2.5ml)
- 2 cups fresh spinach, chopped (about 2.1 oz or 60g)
- 1/4 tsp salt (about 0.05 oz or 1.5g)
- 1/4 tsp freshly ground black pepper (about 0.025 oz or 0.75g)
- 1/2 tsp garlic powder (about 0.05 oz or 1.5g)
- 4 large eggs (about 8 oz or 227g)
- 1 tbsp white vinegar (about 0.5 fl oz or 15ml)
- Optional toppings: crumbled feta cheese, chopped tomatoes, fresh herbs (parsley, chives, or basil)

INSTRUCTIONS

Step 1 | Sauté the Spinach
Heat the olive oil (0.085 fl oz or 2.5ml) in a medium saucepan over medium heat. Add the chopped spinach (2.1 oz or 60g) and sauté until wilted, about 3-4 minutes. Season with salt (0.05 oz or 1.5g), pepper (0.025 oz or 0.75g), and garlic powder (0.05 oz or 1.5g).

Step 2 | Toast the Oats
Stir in the rolled oats (3.2 oz or 90g) and toast lightly with the spinach for 1-2 minutes.

Step 3 | Cook the Oatmeal
Pour in the water or vegetable broth (16 fl oz or 480ml). Increase the heat to bring the mixture to a boil, then reduce heat to a simmer. Cook the oatmeal for about 5-7 minutes, or until the oats are tender and have absorbed most of the liquid.

Step 4 | Poach the Eggs
While the oatmeal is cooking, bring a small pot of water to a gentle boil and add the white vinegar (0.5 fl oz or 15ml). Crack an egg (2 oz or 57g) into a small bowl. Using a spoon, create a whirlpool in the boiling water and gently slide the egg into the center.
Poach the egg for 3-4 minutes or until the whites are set but the yolk remains runny. Use a slotted spoon to remove the egg and place it on a paper towel to drain. Repeat the process with the remaining eggs.

Step 5 | Assemble and Serve
Divide the cooked oatmeal into bowls. Top each bowl with a poached egg, and if desired, add crumbled feta cheese, chopped tomatoes, and fresh herbs.

NOTES

- For a vegan version, omit the eggs and top with a dollop of hummus or avocado slices. Adjust the seasonings as desired, and consider adding a pinch of smoked paprika for a subtle depth of flavor.

- Enjoy this nourishing and versatile dish that pays homage to the essence of Mediterranean cuisine, where simplicity meets wholesome goodness.

BREAKFAST

6 RICOTTA AND BERRY STUFFED FRENCH TOAST, FRANCE

METHOD PAN | **TIME** 15 MINUTE | **SERVING** 4 PERSON | **CALORIES** 415

Elevate your morning with this sumptuous dish that wraps velvety ricotta and vibrant fresh berries in golden-browned French toast. Drizzled with honey and sprinkled with a hint of cinnamon, this dish transforms a classic breakfast into a decadent treat that's perfect for a leisurely morning or a special brunch.

- ✓ Medium bowl
- ✓ Shallow dish
- ✓ Non-stick skillet or griddle
- ✓ Spatula

INGREDIENTS

- 8 slices thick brioche or challah bread
- 1 cup ricotta cheese (about 8.8 oz or 250g)
- 1 cup mixed berries (about 5.3 oz or 150g), strawberries, blueberries, raspberries, more for garnish
- 2 large eggs
- 1/2 cup whole milk (about 4.2 fl oz or 120ml)
- 1 teaspoon vanilla extract (about 0.17 fl oz or 5ml)
- 2 tablespoons granulated sugar (about 0.88 oz or 25g)
- 1/4 teaspoon ground cinnamon (about 0.04 oz or 1g)
- Zest of 1 lemon
- 1 tablespoon unsalted butter (about 0.53 oz or 15g), for cooking
- Honey or maple syrup, for drizzling
- Powdered sugar, for dusting (optional)
- Fresh mint leaves, for garnish (optional)

INSTRUCTIONS

Step 1 | Prepare the Berry Ricotta Filling
In a medium bowl, combine the ricotta cheese (8.8 oz), lemon zest, and 1 tablespoon of sugar (0.44 oz). Gently fold in the mixed berries (5.3 oz), trying not to crush them. Set aside.

Step 2 | Whisk the Egg Mixture
In a shallow dish, whisk together the eggs, milk (4.2 fl oz), vanilla extract (0.17 fl oz), remaining sugar (0.44 oz), and ground cinnamon (0.04 oz) until well combined.

Step 3 | Prep the Bread for Stuffing
Take a slice of bread and spread a generous amount of the ricotta and berry mixture on one side. Top with another slice of bread to create a sandwich. Repeat with the remaining slices to make four stuffed French toasts.

Step 4 | Soak the French Toast
Dip each stuffed bread sandwich into the egg mixture, allowing it to soak for a few seconds on each side.

Step 5 | Cook the French Toast
Heat a large non-stick skillet or griddle over medium heat. Add the butter (0.53 oz) and let it melt. Place the soaked sandwiches in the skillet and cook for about 4-5 minutes on each side, or until golden brown and cooked through.

Step 6 | Serve
Transfer the cooked French toast to plates. Drizzle with honey or maple syrup, dust with powdered sugar if desired, and garnish with additional berries and mint leaves.

NOTES

- For a richer flavor, you can substitute the whole milk with half-and-half or light cream.
- Feel free to swap out the berries for other seasonal fruits or a combination of your favorites.
- If you're serving a crowd, you can keep the cooked French toast warm in an oven set to a low temperature while you finish cooking the rest.

BREAKFAST

7 COUSCOUS BREAKFAST BOWL WITH DATES AND ALMONDS, ALGERIA

INGREDIENTS

- 1 cup couscous (about 6.3 oz or 180g)
- 1 1/4 cups boiling water (about 10.5 fl oz or 300ml)
- 1/2 tsp salt (about 0.09 oz or 2.5g)
- 4 Medjool dates, pitted and chopped (about 3.1 oz or 88g)
- 1/4 cup sliced almonds (about 1 oz or 30g)
- 1/2 tsp cinnamon (about 0.04 oz or 1g)
- 2 tbsp honey (about 1.05 fl oz or 30ml)
- 1/4 cup Greek yogurt (about 2.1 oz or 60g)
- Fresh mint leaves for garnish (optional)

METHOD: MIXING
TIME: 15 MINUTE
SERVING: 2 PERSON
CALORIES: 410

This easy-to-make morning dish is infused with the aromatic warmth of cinnamon, the rich sweetness of dates, and the delightful crunch of toasted almonds. The nutritious and vibrant option offers a deliciously energizing start to your day, perfectly combining heartiness and flavor for a breakfast that's quick to prepare and long to savor.

- ✓ Large bowl
- ✓ Clean kitchen towel or lid
- ✓ Dry skillet
- ✓ Fork

INSTRUCTIONS

Step 1 | Soak the Couscous
Place the couscous (6.3 oz) in a large bowl and sprinkle the salt (0.09 oz) over it. Pour the boiling water (10.5 fl oz) onto the couscous, ensuring it's completely covered. Cover the bowl with a lid or a clean kitchen towel and let it sit for 5 minutes until the water is absorbed.

Step 2 | Toast the Almonds
While the couscous is soaking, toast the sliced almonds (1 oz) in a dry skillet over medium heat for 2-3 minutes, or until they're golden brown and fragrant. Set aside to cool.

Step 3 | Fluff the Couscous
Fluff the couscous gently with a fork to separate the grains and allow any excess steam to escape.

Step 4 | Mix in Ingredients
Stir in the cinnamon (0.04 oz), chopped dates (3.1 oz), and half of the toasted almonds into the couscous, mixing until well combined.

Step 5 | Add Honey
Drizzle honey (1.05 fl oz) over the couscous mixture and fold gently to incorporate the sweet flavor throughout.

Step 6 | Serve
Divide the couscous between two bowls. Top each bowl with a dollop of Greek yogurt (2.1 oz) and sprinkle with the remaining toasted almonds. Garnish with fresh mint leaves if desired.

NOTES

- For a vegan option, substitute honey with maple syrup or agave nectar and use a plant-based yogurt.
- Feel free to add fresh fruits like sliced bananas or berries for additional flavors and textures.
- Couscous can be prepared in advance and stored in the refrigerator for a quick assembly in the morning.

FISH & SEAFOOD

FISH & SEAFOOD

1 MACKEREL WITH HARISSA AND PRESERVED LEMONS, NORTH AFRICA

Delight in succulent mackerel fillets marinated in a vivid harissa paste, oven-baked to tender perfection alongside zesty preserved lemons. Sprinkled with a medley of Mediterranean herbs, this dish offers a vibrant flavor feast that embodies the richness and health benefits of Mediterranean cuisine.

METHOD OVEN | **TIME** 30MINUTE | **SERVING** 4 PERSON | **CALORIES** 290

- Baking sheet
- Parchment paper
- Small mixing bowl
- Measuring spoons
- Knife
- Cutting board

INGREDIENTS

- 4 mackerel fillets (about 24 oz or 680g)
- 2 tbsp harissa paste (1.05 oz or 30g)
- 1 tbsp olive oil (0.5 fl oz or 15ml)
- 2 preserved lemons, thinly sliced
- 4 cloves garlic, minced (0.35 oz or 10g)
- 1 tsp ground cumin (0.07 oz or 2g)
- 1 tsp smoked paprika (0.07 oz or 2g)
- 1/2 tsp sea salt (0.07 oz or 2g)
- 1/4 tsp freshly ground black pepper (0.035 oz or 1g)
- Fresh parsley, chopped for garnish

NOTES

- Adjust the spiciness of the dish by using more or less harissa paste according to your preference.
- If preserved lemons are not available, zest and juice of one fresh lemon can be used as a substitute, although the flavor profile will be slightly different.
- Ensure your mackerel is sustainably sourced to support healthy oceans.

INSTRUCTIONS

Step 1 | Preheat Oven
Preheat your oven to 400°F (200°C).

Step 2 | Prepare Mackerel
Rinse the mackerel fillets (24 oz) and pat them dry with a paper towel.

Step 3 | Mix Marinade
In a small bowl, mix together the harissa paste (1.05 oz), olive oil (0.5 fl oz), minced garlic (0.35 oz), cumin (0.07 oz), smoked paprika (0.07 oz), salt (0.07 oz), and black pepper (0.035 oz) to create a marinade.

Step 4 | Coat Fillets
Lay the mackerel fillets skin-side down on a baking sheet lined with parchment paper. Spread the harissa marinade evenly over each fillet, ensuring they are well-coated.

Step 5 | Add Lemons
Arrange the preserved lemon slices on top of the fillets.

Step 6 | Bake
Place the baking sheet in the oven and bake for 20 minutes, or until the mackerel flakes easily with a fork.

Step 7 | Rest and Garnish
Remove from the oven and let it rest for a couple of minutes. Garnish with fresh parsley before serving.

FISH & SEAFOOD

2 UMBRIAN BAKED TROUT WITH TOMATOES AND OLIVES, ITALY

METHOD — OVEN
TIME — 30 MINUTE
SERVING — 4 PERSON
CALORIES — 380

This dish captures the essence of Umbrian cuisine with its harmonious blend of earthy trout, sweet cherry tomatoes, and savory olives, all baked to perfection. Each bite offers a heart-healthy taste of the Mediterranean, making it a perfect choice for a nourishing dinner.

- ✓ Large baking dish
- ✓ Mixing bowl
- ✓ Cutting board
- ✓ Chef's knife
- ✓ Measuring spoons
- ✓ Measuring cups

INGREDIENTS

- 4 whole trout, cleaned and gutted (about 4 lb or 1.8 kg total)
- 2 cups cherry tomatoes, halved (about 10.6 oz or 300g)
- 1 cup pitted Kalamata olives (about 4.9 oz or 140g)
- 4 cloves garlic, minced (about 0.35 oz or 10g)
- 1 lemon, thinly sliced
- 2 tbsp extra virgin olive oil (about 1 fl oz or 30ml)
- 1 tsp dried oregano (about 0.11 oz or 3g)
- 1 tsp dried thyme (about 0.11 oz or 3g)
- Salt and freshly ground black pepper, to taste
- Fresh parsley, chopped for garnish

INSTRUCTIONS

Step 1 | Preheat Oven
Preheat your oven to 400°F (200°C).

Step 2 | Prepare Trout
Rinse the trout (4 lb) under cold water and pat dry with paper towels. Season the cavity of each trout with salt and pepper.

Step 3 | Stuff Trout
Arrange the trout in a large baking dish. Stuff each trout cavity with lemon slices and a sprinkle of minced garlic (0.35 oz)

Step 4 | Prepare Tomato Mixture
In a bowl, toss the cherry tomatoes (10.6 oz) and olives (4.9 oz) with olive oil (1 fl oz), oregano (0.11 oz), and thyme (0.11 oz). Season with salt and pepper to taste.

Step 5 | Bake
Scatter the tomato and olive mixture around the trout in the baking dish. Drizzle any remaining olive oil from the bowl over the trout. Bake in the preheated oven for 20 minutes, or until the trout flesh flakes easily with a fork.

Step 6 | Rest and Garnish
Remove from the oven and let rest for a couple of minutes before serving. Garnish with fresh parsley and serve immediately.

NOTES

- Ensure trout are thoroughly cleaned and scales removed before cooking.
- Adjust the seasoning to your preference; capers can also be added for an extra burst of flavor.
- Leftovers can be stored in the refrigerator for up to 2 days. Reheat gently to avoid overcooking the fish.
- For a complete Mediterranean meal, serve with a side of quinoa or a fresh green salad.

FISH & SEAFOOD

3   LEMON AND THYME ROASTED SEA BASS, ITALY

INGREDIENTS

- 4 sea bass fillets (24 oz total or 680 grams total, approximately 6 oz or 170 grams each)
- 2 tbsp extra virgin olive oil
  (about 1 fl oz or 30ml)
- 4 cloves garlic, minced (about 0.35 oz or 10g)
- 1 lemon, thinly sliced
- 4 sprigs fresh thyme
- 1 tsp salt (about 0.17 oz or 5g)
- 1/2 tsp black pepper (about 0.09 oz or 2.5g)
- 1/4 cup dry white wine
  (about 2 fl oz or 60ml)
- 1 tbsp unsalted butter (about 0.5 oz or 14g)

METHOD: PAN   **TIME**: 30 MINUTE   **SERVING**: 4 PERSON   **CALORIES**: 280

This dish pairs the delicate texture of sea bass with the bright, zesty flavors of lemon and the aromatic warmth of thyme, creating a meal that's as visually appealing as it is delicious. It's an ideal choice for an elegant dinner that promises to delight and impress your guests.

- ✓ Oven-proof skillet
- ✓ Cutting board
- ✓ Chef's knife
- ✓ Paper towels
- ✓ Measuring cups and spoons

INSTRUCTIONS

Step 1 | Preheat Oven
Preheat your oven to 400°F (200°C).

Step 2 | Prepare Sea Bass
Rinse the sea bass fillets (24 oz) and pat dry with paper towels. Season both sides with salt (0.17 oz) and pepper (0.09 oz).

Step 3 | Sauté Garlic
In a large oven-proof skillet, heat the olive oil (1 fl oz) over medium heat. Add the minced garlic (0.35 oz) and sauté until fragrant, about 1 minute.

Step 4 | Cook Sea Bass
Place the sea bass fillets skin side down in the skillet. Cook for 2-3 minutes until the skin is golden and crisp.

Step 5 | Add Aromatics
Flip the fillets and add the lemon slices and thyme sprigs around the fish in the skillet. Pour the white wine (2 fl oz) into the skillet, then add the butter (0.5 oz) in small pieces around the fish.

Step 6 | Roast
Transfer the skillet to the preheated oven and roast for 12-15 minutes, or until the fish is cooked through and flakes easily with a fork.

Step 7 | Rest and Serve
Remove from the oven and allow the fish to rest for a couple of minutes before serving.

NOTES

- Ensure the sea bass fillets are at room temperature before cooking to ensure even cooking.
- For a more citrusy flavor, zest the lemon before slicing and sprinkle the zest over the fish before roasting.
- If you do not have a skillet that is oven-proof, you can transfer the fish and juices to a preheated baking dish before roasting.
- The cooking time may vary depending on the thickness of the fillets; always check for doneness by using a fork to see if the fish flakes easily.
- Serve with a side of steamed vegetables or a fresh salad for a complete Mediterranean meal.

FISH & SEAFOOD

4 SHRIMP SCAMPI WITH LEMON-GARLIC BUTTER SAUCE, ITALY

Dive into the luxurious simplicity of our Shrimp Scampi, a dish that effortlessly combines the succulent textures of perfectly sautéed shrimp with a sumptuous lemony garlic butter sauce. Ready in minutes, this recipe is ideal for a quick yet impressive dinner, providing a taste of Mediterranean bliss with every bite.

METHOD PAN | **TIME** 15 MINUTE | **SERVING** 4 PERSON | **CALORIES** 286

- Large skillet
- Mixing bowl
- Cutting board
- Chef's knife
- Cooking utensils

INGREDIENTS

- 1 pound medium shrimp, deveined (tail on or peeled) (about 16 oz or 454g)
- ½ teaspoon kosher salt (about 0.11 oz or 3g)
- Fresh ground black pepper, to taste
- ¼ cup finely minced white onion (about 1.4 oz or 40g)
- 6 garlic cloves, finely minced (about 1.06 oz or 30g)
- 2 tablespoons fresh parsley, chopped (about 0.12 oz or 3.5g)
- 2 tablespoons olive oil (about 1 fl oz or 30ml)
- 4 tablespoons salted butter (about 2 oz or 57g)
- ½ cup dry white wine (like Pinot Grigio) or broth (about 4 fl oz or 120ml)
- Zest of 1 lemon
- To serve: 8 ounces Angel Hair Pasta (about 8 oz or 227g), crusty bread, or rice

INSTRUCTIONS

Step 1 | Prepare Shrimp
Thaw the shrimp, if frozen. Pat the shrimp dry (16 oz). In a bowl, sprinkle it with ½ teaspoon kosher salt (0.11 oz) and fresh ground black pepper and stir to combine

Step 2 | Chop Ingredients
Chop the onion (1.4 oz), garlic (1.06 oz), and parsley (0.12 oz).

Step 3 | Sauté Aromatics
In a very large skillet, heat the olive oil (1 fl oz) on medium-high heat. Add the minced onion and garlic and cook for 30 seconds.

Step 4 | Cook Shrimp
Add the shrimp in a single layer (without stacking it) and cook for about 3 minutes, turning halfway through, until just cooked. (The shrimp will continue cooking after removing from the heat.) Remove the shrimp to a bowl while making the sauce.

Step 5 | Make Sauce
In the same skillet, add the butter (2 oz), wine (4 fl oz), lemon zest, and parsley. Simmer for 2 to 3 minutes until slightly thickened.

Step 6 | Combine and Serve
Add the shrimp back to the skillet and rewarm it for a few seconds. Serve immediately, with pasta on the side, rice, or crusty bread (drizzle spoonfuls of the sauce over the shrimp and the pasta on the side).

NOTES

- For larger portions, use up to 1½ pounds of shrimp and ¾ teaspoon of salt, adjusting the batch size for cooking based on your skillet's size.

- You can enhance the flavor by adding ½ teaspoon of garlic powder, and ½ tablespoon each of dried oregano and basil.

- Boil 8 ounces of angel hair pasta for 4 minutes, then cool it under lukewarm water. Dress it with 1 tablespoon of olive oil and ¾ teaspoon of kosher salt.

- Serve the pasta separately from the shrimp to avoid soaking up the sauce; it's challenging to combine them directly in the pan.

FISH & SEAFOOD

5 TUNA MELT STUFFED BELL PEPPERS, CROATIA

METHOD OVEN | **TIME** 25 MINUTE | **SERVING** 4 PERSON | **CALORIES** 205

Transform your weeknight dinners with this healthy option that's both easy and quick to prepare. These low-carb stuffed peppers burst with the flavors of creamy tuna salad and melted cheese, making them a perfect meal that's ready in under 30 minutes.

- ✓ Rectangular ceramic 13x9 baking dish
- ✓ Mixing bowl set

INGREDIENTS

- 2 bell peppers, halved and cored (approximately 14 oz or 400g total)
- 2 cans of 4.5-ounce Solid Yellowfin Tuna in Extra Virgin Olive Oil (total 9 oz or 255g)
- 2 celery stalks, minced (approximately 3.5 oz or 100g)
- 4 green onions, sliced (greens and whites separated) (approximately 1.5 oz or 43g)
- ⅓ cup 2% Greek yogurt (about 2.7 oz or 77g)
- 2 tablespoons lemon juice (about 1 fl oz or 30ml)
- 1 tablespoon Dijon mustard (about 0.5 oz or 15g)
- ¼ teaspoon salt (about 0.05 oz or 1.5g)
- ¼ teaspoon black pepper (about 0.05 oz or 1.5g)
- ¼ cup shredded cheddar cheese (about 1 oz or 28g)

INSTRUCTIONS

Step 1 | Preheat the Oven
Preheat the oven to 425°F (220°C).

Step 2 | Bake the Peppers
Place the green pepper halves (14 oz) in an oven-safe baking dish and bake until the peppers soften, about 15 minutes.

Step 3 | Prepare the Tuna Salad
In a mixing bowl, stir together the Greek yogurt (2.7 oz), lemon juice (1 fl oz), Dijon mustard (0.5 oz), salt (0.05 oz), and black pepper (0.05 oz) until well combined. Add the tuna (9 oz), along with the celery (3.5 oz) and most of the green onions (1.5 oz, leaving some for garnish). Gently stir until well combined.tuna (9 oz), along with the celery (3.5 oz) and most of the green onions (1.5 oz, leaving some for garnish). Gently stir until well combined.

Step 4 | Stuff the Peppers
Scoop the tuna salad into the crevice of the four baked pepper halves and sprinkle the cheddar cheese (1 oz) on top. Return the peppers to the oven until the cheese melts, about 5 more minutes.

Step 5 | Garnish and Serve
Garnish with extra green onions and serve warm.

NOTES

- **Storage:** Store any leftovers in an airtight container. They will last about 3-4 days in the fridge.

FISH & SEAFOOD

6 TUNA STEAK WITH OPTIONAL GARLIC HERB SAUCE, ITALY

INGREDIENTS

- 2 tuna steaks, 8 ounces each (total 16 oz or 454g, sashimi grade recommended; wild caught if possible)
- ½ tablespoon neutral oil (about 0.25 fl oz or 7.5ml)
- ¾ teaspoon kosher salt (about 0.05 oz or 1.5g)
- Fresh ground black pepper, to taste
- For serving: Garlic Herb Sauce (optional)

METHOD PAN | **TIME** 15 MINUTE | **SERVING** 2 PERSON | **CALORIES** 175

Perfect the tuna steak with this straightforward recipe that promises a sashimi-grade sear in just minutes. Ideal for a gourmet meal that's both quick and impressive, this tuna steak recipe is a delightful showcase of quality and simplicity.

- ✓ Medium skillet
- ✓ Food thermometer
- ✓ Cutting board
- ✓ Knife

INSTRUCTIONS

Step 1 | Prepare the Tuna
Allow the tuna steak to come to room temperature by letting it stand for at least 20 minutes.

Step 2 | Season the Tuna
Pat the tuna dry (16 oz). Sprinkle it liberally with kosher salt (0.05 oz) and fresh ground black pepper on both sides to get a nice even coating.

Step 3 | Heat the Skillet
Heat the oil (0.25 fl oz) in a medium skillet over medium-high heat.

Step 4 | Cook the Tuna
Add the tuna steak and cook for 1 to 2 minutes per side (2 to 4 minutes total), until lightly browned on the outside but still rare on the inside. For a medium-rare tuna steak, the internal temperature should be 130 degrees Fahrenheit when measured with a food thermometer at the thickest point.

Step 5 | Rest and Serve
Cool for 2 minutes. Then slice the tuna against the grain into ½-inch slices and serve immediately, with the sauce if desired.

NOTES

- Frozen tuna is acceptable; just ensure to thaw it in the refrigerator before cooking.

FISH & SEAFOOD

7 CASSEROLE FISH WITH ONIONS AND TOMATOES, GREECE

Psari Plaki, a traditional Greek dish that combines tender white fish with a rich tomato and onion sauce, seasoned with fragrant herbs. This comforting baked fish recipe is perfect for infusing a weeknight dinner with simplicity and elegance. Serve it alongside rustic bread or over your favorite grains for a fulfilling meal.

METHOD OVEN | **TIME** 25 MINUTE | **SERVING** 6 PERSON | **CALORIES** 160

- Oven-safe pan or large skillet
- Wooden spoon
- Knife
- Cutting board
- Baking dish

INGREDIENTS

— For the Sauce:

- 2 tablespoons extra virgin olive oil (1 fl oz or 30 ml)
- 1 large yellow onion, halved and thinly sliced (about 6 oz or 170g)
- 2 large garlic cloves, minced (about 0.7 oz or 20g)
- 1 (28-ounce) can whole peeled tomatoes (28 oz or 794g)
- 2 teaspoons dried oregano (about 0.18 oz or 5g)
- Black pepper, to taste

— For the Fish:

- 2 pounds white fish fillet, such as halibut or cod (32 oz or 907g)
- Kosher salt, to taste
- ½ teaspoon dried oregano (about 0.05 oz or 1.5g)
- 1 teaspoon sweet paprika (about 0.1 oz or 3g)
- ½ teaspoon ground cumin (about 0.05 oz or 1.5g)
- 2 lemons, divided (about 10 oz or 284g total)
- ¼ cup fresh parsley, chopped (about 0.2 oz or 6g)

INSTRUCTIONS

Step 1 | Heat the Oven
Preheat the oven to 400°F (200°C) and position a rack in the middle

Step 2 | Make the Sauce
In a large oven-safe pan, heat the olive oil (1 fl oz) over medium-high heat until shimmering. Add the sliced onions (6 oz) with a pinch of kosher salt. Cook, stirring regularly, until the onions soften and turn golden-brown, about 7 minutes. Add the minced garlic (0.7 oz) and stir briefly before adding the canned tomatoes (28 oz). Break the tomatoes up with a wooden spoon. Season with more salt, oregano (0.18 oz), and black pepper. Bring to a boil, then reduce the heat and simmer for 10 to 15 minutes.

Step 3 | Season the Fish
Pat the fish dry (32 oz) and season both sides with kosher salt, oregano (0.05 oz), paprika (0.1 oz), and cumin (0.05 oz). Squeeze one lemon (5 oz) over the fish.

Step 4 | Combine Sauce and Fish
Once the sauce is ready, nestle the fish in the sauce, scooping some sauce over the top of the fish.

Step 5 | Bake
Transfer the pan to the center rack of the oven and bake until the fish turns opaque white and flakes easily with a fork, approximately 15 to 25 minutes.

Step 6 | Serve
Slice the remaining lemon into wedges. Sprinkle the baked fish with fresh parsley (0.2 oz) and serve with the lemon wedges on the side.

NOTES

- **Storage:** Store any leftovers in an airtight container in the fridge for up to 2 days.

- **Variation:** For a zestier flavor, add a pinch of chili flakes to the tomato sauce.

MEAT

MEAT

1 ROASTED LAMB AND POTATOES, CRETE

METHOD — OVEN
TIME — 1 HOUR 30 MINUTE
SERVING — 6 PERSON
CALORIES — 638

Immerse in the robust flavors of the Mediterranean with this hearty lamb bake. Juicy lamb pieces are surrounded by seasoned potatoes and zucchini, all expertly roasted to bring out their rich, comforting flavors—ideal for cozy family dinners.

- Oven
- Baking dish
- Mixing bowl
- Knife

INGREDIENTS

- Lamb: 2 pounds, bone-in (32 oz or 907g)
- Potatoes: 6, peeled, quartered (24 oz or 680g)
- Zucchini: 2, quartered (14 oz or 400g)
- Tomato: 1, grated (4 oz or 113g)
- Garlic: 3 cloves, minced (0.5 oz or 15g)
- Dried Oregano: 1 tbsp (0.5 oz or 14g)
- Extra Virgin Olive Oil: 3/4 cup (6 fl oz or 177 ml)
- Salt and Pepper: to taste

INSTRUCTIONS

Step 1 | Preheat Oven
Set to 400°F (204°C).

Step 2 | Prepare Lamb
Cut lamb into 4 pieces (each 8 oz or 227g).

Step 3 | Combine Ingredients
In a baking dish, mix lamb, potatoes (24 oz or 680g), zucchini (14 oz or 400g), tomato (4 oz or 113g), garlic (0.5 oz or 15g), oregano (0.5 oz or 14g), olive oil (6 fl oz or 177 ml), salt, and pepper.

Step 4 | Arrange for Roasting
Place lamb on top in the dish.

Step 5 | Bake
Cook for 1 hour 15 minutes at 400°F. Midway, flip lamb and stir vegetables.

NOTES

- **Side Suggestions:** Serve with a green salad or crusty bread for soaking up the juices.
- **Storage:** Leftovers keep well in the refrigerator for a few days, making for flavorful reheats.

MEAT

BEEF TENDERLOIN ROAST RECIPE, LEBANON

INGREDIENTS

- Beef Tenderloin: 3 lbs, center-cut, excess fat trimmed (48 oz or 1360g)
- Kosher Salt: to taste
- Black Pepper: to taste
- Extra Virgin Olive Oil
- Optional: Chermoula sauce for serving (Spices & Sauces chapter)
- Optional: Pomegranate seeds for garnish

METHOD OVEN
TIME 4 HOUR
SERVING 8 PERSON
CALORIES 465

Indulge in the decadent flavors of this Beef Tenderloin Roast, delivering a succulent, perfectly cooked roast with a golden-brown crust. This simple method ensures a tender and juicy centerpiece that is ideal for special occasions, offering unforgettable flavor and texture with minimal stress.

- ✓ Kitchen twine
- ✓ Large sheet pan
- ✓ Tongs
- ✓ Oven-safe wire cooling rack

INSTRUCTIONS

Step 1 | Prep the Tenderloin
Season with kosher salt and black pepper. Tie with kitchen twine at 1-inch intervals (48 oz or 1360g).

Step 2 | Air Dry
Place on a wire rack set over a sheet pan and refrigerate uncovered overnight. If short on time, allow 30 minutes to 1 hour.

Step 3 | Start Slow-Roasting
Position oven racks and preheat to 225°F (107°C). Slow-roast on the center rack until it reaches 10°F below your desired doneness, approximately 2-3 hours.

Step 4 | Broil for Crust
Increase to broil. Brush with olive oil and broil, turning for even browning (about 2 minutes).

Step 5 | Rest
Let it rest 15-20 minutes after removing from the oven.

Step 6 | Prepare Chermoula
If using, prepare chermoula sauce.

Step 7 | Serve
Remove twine, slice, and serve with optional chermoula sauce and pomegranate seeds.

NOTES

- **Versatility**: Substitute chermoula with other robust sauces.
- **Presentation**: Enhance with fresh herbs or additional garnishes for visual appeal.
- **Storage**: Leftovers can be refrigerated and used within a few days, maintaining delicious flavor.

MEAT

3 GRILLED LAMB CHOPS WITH ROSEMARY, CORSICA

INGREDIENTS

- **Lamb Chops:** 8 pieces, 1-inch thick each (2 lbs or 0.9 kg total)
- **Olive Oil:** 2 tbsp (1 fl oz or 30 ml)
- **Garlic:** 4 cloves, minced
- **Fresh Rosemary:** 2 tbsp, finely chopped (0.5 oz or 15g)
- **Lemon:** Zest and juice (2 tbsp or 30 ml juice)
- **Sea Salt:** 1 tsp (5g)
- **Black Pepper:** ½ tsp, freshly ground (2.5g)

METHOD	TIME	SERVING	CALORIES
GRILL	25 MINUTE	4 PERSON	410

Immerse yourself in the vibrant, herbaceous flavors of Corsica with these Grilled Lamb Chops. Marinated in fresh rosemary, garlic, and lemon, these chops offer a delightful taste of the island's rustic and aromatic culinary style.

- ✓ Grill
- ✓ Shallow dish or resealable plastic bag
- ✓ Small bowl
- ✓ Tongs

INSTRUCTIONS

Step 1 | Marinade Preparation
Combine olive oil, garlic, rosemary, lemon zest, lemon juice, salt, and pepper in a small bowl.

Step 2 | Marinate Chops
Place lamb chops in a dish or bag. Cover with marinade and refrigerate for 2 hours or overnight.

Step 3 | Grilling
Preheat grill to medium-high. Remove chops from marinade and grill 4-5 minutes per side for medium-rare.

Step 4 | Rest and Serve
Let chops rest for 5 minutes then serve, garnished with rosemary if desired.

NOTES

- **Temperature Tip:** Bring chops to room temperature before grilling for even cooking.
- **Doneness:** Adjust grilling time based on the thickness of chops and desired doneness.
- **Flavor Tip:** Use fresh rosemary for the best flavor.

MEAT

4 OSSO BUCO WITH GREMOLATA AND SAFFRON RISOTTO, ITALY

Indulge in Milanese elegance with Osso Buco and Saffron Risotto, a sophisticated dish perfect for special occasions. Braised veal shanks and aromatic risotto are enriched with vibrant gremolata, delivering a luxurious dining experience.

METHOD OVEN
TIME 2 HOUR 30 MINUTE
SERVING 4 PERSON
CALORIES 980

- Dutch oven or heavy-bottomed pot
- Medium saucepan
- Knife
- Measuring tools
- Kitchen twine
- Cutting board

INGREDIENTS

— Osso Buco:
- Veal Shanks: 4 pieces, 1 inch thick, tied
- Olive Oil: 2 tbsp
- All-Purpose Flour: 1 cup (for dredging)
- Onion: 1 large, finely chopped
- Carrots: 2, finely chopped
- Celery: 2 stalks, finely chopped
- Garlic: 4 cloves, minced
- Dry White Wine: 1 cup
- Beef Broth: 2 cups
- Diced Tomatoes: 1 can (14 oz)
- Tomato Paste: 2 tbsp
- Fresh Thyme: 3 sprigs
- Bay Leaves: 2

— Gremolata:
- Lemon Zest: From 1 lemon
- Parsley: 2 tbsp, chopped
- Garlic: 2 cloves, minced

— Saffron Risotto:
- Onion: 1 small, finely chopped
- Unsalted Butter: 2 tbsp
- Arborio Rice: 1 1/2 cups
- Dry White Wine: 1/2 cup
- Warm Chicken Broth: 5 cups
- Saffron Threads: A pinch
- Parmesan Cheese: 1/2 cup, grated

INSTRUCTIONS

Step 1 | Preheat Oven
Set to 325°F (163°C). Season and flour veal shanks.

Step 2 | Brown Veal
In a Dutch oven, sear veal in hot oil; set aside.

Step 3 | Sauté Vegetables
Cook onions, carrots, celery, and garlic until soft.

Step 4 | Deglaze and Braise
Add wine, then broth, tomatoes, and herbs. Return veal, cover, and oven-braise (1.5-2 hrs).

Step 5 | Prepare Gremolata
Mix lemon zest, parsley, and garlic.

Step 6 | Make Risotto
Sauté onion in butter, add rice and wine, then gradually broth and saffron. Stir in Parmesan.

Step 7 | Serve
Top Osso Buco with gremolata and serve with risotto.

NOTES

- **Substitute Veal:** Use pork or beef shanks if preferred.
- **Serving Suggestion:** Pair with steamed greens like asparagus.
- **Storage:** Refrigerate leftovers to maintain flavor.

MEAT

5 BEEF PICCATA, ITALY

METHOD — SKILLET
TIME — 20 MINUTE
SERVING — 4 PERSON
CALORIES — 450

Italian Beef Piccata is an elegant dish that features tender beef steaks, capers, and a vibrant lemon sauce. Quick to prepare, this dish delivers sophisticated flavors and is perfect for an impressive yet easy dinner.

- Skillet
- Cutting board
- Plate (for dredging)
- Measuring cups and spoons
- Knife

INGREDIENTS

- 4 beef tenderloin steaks, pounded thin (about 2 lbs or 900g total)
- 1/4 cup flour (about 1 oz or 28g) (for dredging)
- 2 tbsp capers (1 fl oz or 30ml)
- Juice of 1 lemon (about 2 tbsp or 30ml)
- 1/2 cup beef broth (4 fl oz or 120ml)
- 3 tbsp olive oil (1.5 fl oz or 45ml)
- Salt and pepper to taste

INSTRUCTIONS

Step 1 | Prepare the steaks
Season the beef tenderloin steaks (2 lbs or 900g) with salt and pepper. Lightly dredge each steak in flour (1/4 cup or 28g), shaking off any excess.

Step 2 | Cook the steaks
Heat olive oil (3 tbsp or 45ml) in a skillet over medium-high heat. Add the steaks and cook for about 2-3 minutes on each side, or until golden and cooked to desired doneness. Remove from the skillet and keep warm.

Step 3 | Make the sauce
In the same skillet, add lemon juice (2 tbsp or 30ml), capers (2 tbsp or 30ml), and beef broth (1/2 cup or 120ml). Bring to a simmer, scraping up any browned bits from the bottom of the pan. Reduce the sauce until slightly thickened, about 3-4 minutes.

Step 4 | Serve
Return the steaks to the skillet, coat them with the sauce, and heat through. Serve the steaks with the sauce poured over them.

NOTES

- If beef tenderloin is unavailable, veal or chicken cutlets can be used as a substitute for a variation of this recipe.
- Capers add a briny depth to the sauce, but if you prefer a milder flavor, they can be rinsed before adding to the pan.
- Pair this dish with a side of steamed green beans or a light salad for a balanced meal.
- Leftover Piccata makes excellent sandwich fillings when sliced thinly.

MEAT

6 LAMB MEATBALLS WITH TZATZIKI AND POMEGRANATE GLAZE, GREECE

INGREDIENTS

— For the Lamb Meatballs:
- 1 lb ground lamb (about 16 oz or 450g)
- 1/4 cup breadcrumbs (about 1 oz or 30g)
- 1 large egg
- 2 cloves garlic, minced (about 1 tbsp or 15ml)
- 1/4 cup finely chopped onion (about 2 oz or 60g)
- 1/4 cup fresh parsley, chopped (about 1 oz or 30g)
- 1 tsp ground cumin (5ml)
- 1 tsp smoked paprika (5ml)
- 1/2 tsp salt (2.5ml)
- 1/2 tsp black pepper (2.5ml)
- 1 tbsp olive oil (15ml)
- Tzatziki (Spices & Sauces Chapter)
- Pomegranate Glaze: (Spices & Sauces Chapter)

METHOD OVEN
TIME 45 MINUTE
SERVING 4 PERSON
CALORIES 410

Explore the rich culinary traditions of the Mediterranean with these Lamb Meatballs, enhanced by the cool freshness of tzatziki and the sweet tartness of pomegranate glaze. This dish combines succulent flavors with vibrant aromas, perfect for a sophisticated appetizer or a main course.

- ✓ Large mixing bowl
- ✓ Baking sheet
- ✓ Grater
- ✓ Small saucepan
- ✓ Parchment paper

INSTRUCTIONS

Step 1 | Prepare for baking
Preheat your oven to 400°F (200°C). Line a baking sheet with parchment paper.

Step 2 | Make meatballs
In a large bowl, combine ground lamb (1 lb or 450g), breadcrumbs (1/4 cup or 30g), egg, minced garlic (1 tbsp or 15ml), chopped onion (1/4 cup or 60g), chopped parsley (1/4 cup or 30g), ground cumin (1 tsp or 5ml), smoked paprika (1 tsp or 5ml), salt (1/2 tsp or 2.5ml), and black pepper (1/2 tsp or 2.5ml). Mix well.

Step 3 | Shape and bake meatballs
Form the mixture into 1-inch (2.5 cm) meatballs and place them on the prepared baking sheet. Drizzle with olive oil (1 tbsp or 15ml). Bake for 20-25 minutes, until browned and cooked through.

Step 4 | Serve
Place cooked meatballs on a plate, drizzle with pomegranate glaze, and serve with tzatziki on the side.

NOTES

- For a lighter option, substitute ground lamb with ground turkey or chicken.
- Perfect for a mezze platter; consider making smaller meatballs and pairing with additional Mediterranean sides.
- Ensure the pomegranate glaze is cool before drizzling to ensure the perfect consistency.

MEAT

7 | RABBIT STEW WITH VEGETABLES AND WHITE WINE, IBIZA

INGREDIENTS

- 1 whole rabbit, cut into pieces (about 3-4 pounds or 1.4-1.8 kg)
- 2 tbsp olive oil (30 ml)
- 1 large onion, diced (about 1 cup or 150 g)
- 4 cloves garlic, minced
- 2 carrots, sliced (about 1 cup or 130 g)
- 2 stalks celery, sliced (about 1/2 cup or 60 g)
- 1 red bell pepper, diced (about 1 cup or 150 g)
- 1 cup white wine (240 ml)
- 2 cups chicken broth (480 ml)
- 1 can diced tomatoes (14 oz or 400 g)
- 1 tsp fresh thyme leaves
- 1 bay leaf
- Salt and pepper to taste
- 2 tbsp fresh parsley, chopped (for garnish)

METHOD POT
TIME 2 HOUR 30 MINUTE
SERVING 4 PERSON
CALORIES 450

Delve into the rich flavors of the Mediterranean with this hearty Ibizan Rabbit Stew. A traditional dish from the island of Ibiza, it combines tender rabbit meat with fresh vegetables and aromatic herbs, all simmered in a robust white wine. This stew captures the essence of Ibiza's culinary heritage.

- ✓ Cutting board
- ✓ Wooden spoon
- ✓ Large pot
- ✓ Chef's knife

INSTRUCTIONS

Step 1 | Season the rabbit
Season rabbit pieces with salt and pepper to enhance their flavor.

Step 2 | Brown the rabbit
In a large pot, heat olive oil (2 tbsp or 30 ml) over medium-high heat. Add rabbit pieces and brown on all sides to seal in juices. Remove and set aside.

Step 3 | Sauté vegetables
In the same pot, add diced onion (1 cup or 150g), minced garlic, sliced carrots (1 cup or 130g), sliced celery (1/2 cup or 60g), and diced red bell pepper (1 cup or 150g). Sauté until vegetables are softened, about 5 minutes.

Step 4 | Deglaze and simmer
Pour in white wine (1 cup or 240ml) to deglaze the pot, scraping up any browned bits from the bottom. Return the browned rabbit to the pot. Add chicken broth (2 cups or 480ml), diced tomatoes, fresh thyme, and bay leaf.
Bring to a boil, then reduce heat to low and simmer, covered, for 1.5 to 2 hours, or until the rabbit is tender.

Step 5 | Finish and serve
Adjust seasoning with salt and pepper. Remove the bay leaf. Garnish with fresh parsley and serve hot.

NOTES

- If rabbit is not available, chicken thighs are an excellent substitute and will similarly absorb the rich flavors of the stew.

- Serve this stew with crusty bread or over cooked rice to soak up the delicious sauce, enhancing the dining experience.

- For a thicker stew, mix a tablespoon of cornstarch with water and add it to the stew during the last 30 minutes of cooking.

MEAT

8 | LAMB STEW WITH HERBS AND WHITE BEANS, CORSICA

Experience a taste of Corsica with this hearty lamb stew. Combining succulent lamb shoulder with white beans and aromatic herbs, this stew encapsulates the essence of Mediterranean cooking. Perfect for a wholesome meal, it offers a nutritious blend of protein, fiber, and herbs that comfort and satisfy.

METHOD STOVETOP **TIME** 1 HOUR 50 MINUTE **SERVING** 6 PERSON **CALORIES** 450

- Large pot or Dutch oven
- Wooden spoon
- Knife
- Measuring cups and spoons
- Kitchen twine
- Cutting board

INGREDIENTS

- Lamb Shoulder: 2 pounds, cut into 2-inch pieces
- Olive Oil: 1 tablespoon
- Onion: 1 large, diced
- Garlic: 3 cloves, minced
- Sea Salt: 1 teaspoon
- Black Pepper: 1/2 teaspoon
- Tomato Paste: 1 tablespoon
- Dry White Wine: 1 cup
- Chicken or Vegetable Broth: 3 cups
- Fresh Herbs: Rosemary (2 sprigs), Thyme (2 sprigs), Bay Leaves (2)
- White Beans: 2 cups, canned, drained and rinsed
- Cherry Tomatoes: 1 cup, halved
- Lemon: Zest of 1 lemon
- Parsley: Fresh, chopped for garnish

NOTES

- **Thicken Stew:** For a thicker texture, mash some beans before adding.
- **Using Dried Beans:** Pre-cook soaked dried beans before adding.
- **Storage:** Store leftovers in the fridge for up to 3 days or freeze for up to 3 months.
- **Serving Suggestion:** Serve with crusty bread or a side salad.

INSTRUCTIONS

Step 1 | Brown Lamb
Heat olive oil in a Dutch oven. Brown lamb pieces on all sides (5-7 mins). Remove and set aside.

Step 2 | Sauté Aromatics
Reduce to medium heat. Sauté onion and garlic until translucent (3-4 mins).

Step 3 | Add Seasonings
Mix in salt, pepper, and tomato paste. Cook for 1 minute.

Step 4 | Deglaze
Pour in white wine, scraping up any bits from the pot.

Step 5 | Simmer Lamb
Return lamb to pot. Add broth. Bring to a simmer.

Step 6 | Herb Bundle
Tie rosemary, thyme, and bay leaves with twine. Add to pot.

Step 7 | Slow Cook
Cover and simmer on low for 1 hour until lamb is tender.

Step 8 | Add Beans and Tomatoes
Add white beans and tomatoes. Simmer uncovered for 30 minutes.

Step 9 | Final Touches
Remove herb bundle. Stir in lemon zest. Adjust seasoning.

Step 10 | Garnish and Serve
Garnish with parsley.

PASTA

PASTA

1 ARTICHOKE AND OLIVE PASTA WITH LEMON AND GARLIC, ITALY

METHOD POT | **TIME** 35 MINUTE | **SERVING** 4 PERSON | **CALORIES** 420

A delightful medley of juicy artichokes, rich Kalamata olives, zestful lemon, and robust garlic come together to create a dish that not only captivates the senses but also enriches your dining experience with its bold and sunny flavors.

- Large pot
- Colander
- Large skillet
- Cheese grater
- Measuring cups and spoons

INGREDIENTS

- 12 ounces pasta (about 340g)
- 1 can artichoke hearts, drained and quartered
- 1 cup Kalamata olives, pitted and halved (about 150g)
- 3 tbsp extra virgin olive oil (45ml)
- 4 cloves garlic, minced
- Zest of 1 lemon
- 2 tbsp fresh lemon juice (30ml)
- 1 tsp red pepper flakes (optional)
- Salt and freshly ground black pepper, to taste
- 1/4 cup fresh parsley, chopped (about 15g)
- Grated Parmesan cheese, for serving

INSTRUCTIONS

Step 1 | Prepare the Pasta
Cook pasta in a large pot of salted boiling water until al dente. Before draining, reserve 1 cup (240ml) of the pasta water.

Step 2 | Sauté Garlic and Spices
In a large skillet, heat olive oil (3 tbsp) over medium. Add minced garlic and red pepper flakes, sautéing until fragrant (about 1 minute).

Step 3 | Add Artichokes and Olives
Incorporate artichoke hearts into the skillet, cooking until golden (2-3 minutes). Mix in halved Kalamata olives and lemon zest.

Step 4 | Combine and Season
Reduce heat, add cooked pasta, and toss. If needed, loosen sauce with reserved pasta water. Add lemon juice and season with salt and pepper.

Step 5 | Final Touches
Remove from heat, stir in chopped parsley, and serve with grated Parmesan.

NOTES

- Adjust red pepper to your liking.
- Refrigerate leftovers in an airtight container for up to 3 days.
- Add grilled chicken or shrimp for extra protein.

PASTA

2 PASTA WITH ROASTED TOMATOES AND ALMOND PESTO, ITALY

INGREDIENTS

— Roasted Tomatoes

- 2 lbs cherry tomatoes, halved (about 900g)
- 2 tbsp extra-virgin olive oil (30ml)
- 1 tsp sea salt (5g)
- 1/2 tsp freshly ground black pepper (1g)

— Almond Pesto

- 1 cup almonds, toasted (143g)
- 2 cups fresh basil leaves
- 2 cloves garlic
- 1/2 cup extra-virgin olive oil (120ml)
- 1/2 cup grated Parmesan cheese
- Juice of 1 lemon

— Pasta

- 1 lb whole wheat pasta (about 454g)
- Salt for pasta water

METHOD: POT
TIME: 35 MINUTE
SERVING: 4 PERSON
CALORIES: 650

Exquisite Pasta with Roasted Tomatoes and Almond Pesto. The dish brilliantly merges the sweet, intensified flavor of roasted cherry tomatoes with a homemade almond pesto, delivering a rich and savory taste that is quintessentially Mediterranean and deeply satisfying.

- ✓ Large pot
- ✓ Baking sheet
- ✓ Oven
- ✓ Food processor
- ✓ Colander
- ✓ Mixing bowls

INSTRUCTIONS

Step 1 | Roast Tomatoes
Preheat oven to 400°F (200°C). Spread cherry tomatoes (2 lbs) on a parchment-lined baking sheet. Drizzle with olive oil (2 tbsp), season with salt (1 tsp) and pepper (1/2 tsp). Roast for 25-30 minutes until caramelized.

Step 2 | Prepare Almond Pesto
In a food processor, pulse toasted almonds, basil leaves, and garlic until chopped. Gradually add olive oil (1/2 cup) to achieve a smooth paste. Incorporate Parmesan cheese and lemon juice, seasoning with salt and pepper.

Step 3 | Cook Pasta
Boil pasta in salted water to al dente, reserve 1 cup pasta water before draining. Toss pasta with almond pesto, adjusting consistency with pasta water if needed.

Step 4 | Combine and Serve
Fold roasted tomatoes into the pasta. Serve garnished with extra Parmesan and basil leaves.

NOTES

- Toast almonds at 350°F (175°C) for 8-10 minutes until golden.
- Opt for whole wheat pasta for added fiber, or use your preferred type.
- Store any leftover pesto in the fridge, it's excellent as a spread or dip.

PASTA

3 COUSCOUS WITH ROASTED VEGETABLES AND LEMON DRESSING, ISRAEL

INGREDIENTS

— Vegetables:
- 1 cup Israeli couscous (about 200g)
- 2 cups water (about 473ml)
- 1 medium zucchini, diced (about 1 cup/140g)
- 1 red bell pepper, diced (about 150g)
- 1 yellow bell pepper, diced (about 150g)
- 1 red onion, chopped (about 160g)
- 2 tbsp olive oil (about 30ml)
- 1 tsp salt (about 5g)
- 1/2 tsp black pepper (about 2g)
- 1/4 cup fresh parsley, chopped (about 15g)
- 1/4 cup fresh mint, chopped (about 15g)

— Lemon Dressing:
- 1/4 cup extra virgin olive oil (about 60ml)
- 2 tbsp fresh lemon juice (about 30ml)
- 1 tsp lemon zest (about 5g)
- 1 clove garlic, minced (about 5g)
- 1/2 tsp honey (about 2.5ml)

METHOD POT
TIME 35 MINUTE
SERVING 4 PERSON
CALORIES 330

This couscous dish features perfectly roasted vegetables and plump pearls of couscous, all brought together with a tangy lemon dressing. Ideal for a nutritious light lunch or a robust side dish, this dish is a celebration of texture and taste.

- ✓ Oven
- ✓ Baking sheet
- ✓ Parchment paper
- ✓ Medium saucepan
- ✓ Large bowl
- ✓ Small bowl
- ✓ Whisk

INSTRUCTIONS

Step 1 | Prepare Vegetables
Preheat oven to 425°F (220°C). Toss zucchini, both bell peppers, and red onion with olive oil (2 tbsp), salt (1 tsp), and black pepper (1/2 tsp). Spread on a parchment-lined baking sheet. Roast for 20 minutes until caramelized, stirring halfway.

Step 2 | Cook Couscou
Boil water (2 cups) in a medium saucepan. Add couscous, cook 10-12 minutes until al dente. Drain and cool.

Step 3 | Make Dressing
Whisk olive oil, lemon juice, zest, garlic, and honey in a small bowl. Season with salt and pepper.

Step 4 | Combine and Serve
Mix roasted vegetables, couscous, parsley, and mint in a large bowl. Dress with lemon dressing. Adjust seasoning and serve chilled or at room temperature.

NOTES

- Switch to quinoa or rice for a gluten-free version.
- Add chickpeas or feta for extra protein.
- Store up to 3 days refrigerated.
- For a nuttier couscous, toast it dry before boiling.

PASTA

4 SPAGHETTI WITH FRESH SARDINES AND WILD FENNEL, SICILY

This dish captures the essence of Mediterranean culinary traditions, blending the briny zest of sardines with the fragrant allure of wild fennel. It's a harmonious fusion that not only tantalizes the taste buds but also evokes the serene, sunlit coasts of the Mediterranean. Each bite is a sensory celebration, promising both satisfaction and a touch of coastal magic.

METHOD
POT

TIME
50 MINUTE

SERVING
4 PERSON

CALORIES
580

- ✓ Large pot
- ✓ Colander
- ✓ Spatula
- ✓ Large skillet
- ✓ Cutting board
- ✓ Zester
- ✓ Chef's knife
- ✓ Measuring cups and spoons

INGREDIENTS

- Spaghetti, 12 oz (340 g)
- Fresh sardines, cleaned and filleted, 1 lb (454 g)
- Wild fennel fronds, roughly chopped, 1 cup
- Extra virgin olive oil, 3 tbsp (45 ml)
- Garlic cloves, finely sliced, 3
- Red chili flakes, 1/2 tsp (2.5 g)
- Lemon zest, from 1 lemon
- White wine, 1/2 cup (120 ml)
- Pine nuts, toasted, 1/4 cup
- Raisins, 1/4 cup
- Salt, to taste
- Freshly ground black pepper, to taste
- Reserved pasta water, 1/2 cup (120 ml)

INSTRUCTIONS

Step 1 | Prepare Ingredients
Begin by cleaning and filleting the sardines (1 lb or 454 g). Roughly chop the wild fennel fronds and slice the garlic cloves. Zest the lemon.

Step 2 | Cook Spaghetti
In a large pot of salted boiling water, cook the spaghetti (12 oz or 340 g) according to package instructions until al dente. Before draining, reserve 1/2 cup (120 ml) of the pasta water.

Step 3 | Sauté Aromatics
In a large skillet, heat the olive oil (3 tbsp or 45 ml). Add the garlic slices and red chili flakes (1/2 tsp or 2.5 g), sautéing until fragrant.

Step 4 | Add Sardines
Increase heat and add the sardine fillets, breaking them into smaller pieces. Cook until starting to brown, about 3 minutes.

Step 5 | Deglaze with Wine
Add white wine (1/2 cup or 120 ml) and reduce by half.

Step 6 | Incorporate Fennel and Seasonings
Stir in the wild fennel fronds, lemon zest, toasted pine nuts, and raisins. Season with salt and pepper.

Step 7 | Combine with Spaghetti
Toss the drained spaghetti with the sardine mixture, adding reserved pasta water (1/2 cup or 120 ml) if needed.

Step 8 | Serve
Plate the spaghetti, garnishing with additional wild fennel fronds if desired.

NOTES

- Substitute wild fennel with fennel seeds if unavailable.
- For an extra fresh twist, add a squeeze of lemon juice before serving.
- Ensure sardines are fresh for optimal flavor; thaw properly if using frozen.

PASTA

5 RICOTTA AND SAFFRON DUMPLINGS (MALLOREDDUS), SARDINIA

METHOD
POT

TIME
35 MINUTE

SERVING
4 PERSON

CALORIES
420

In Sardinian culinary tradition with these Ricotta and Saffron Dumplings, known as Malloreddus. This dish features the rich textures of semolina and ricotta enhanced by the luxurious aroma of saffron, offering a taste of the island's rustic yet refined flavor palette.

- ✓ Large mixing bowl
- ✓ Fork or gnocchi board
- ✓ Large pot for boiling
- ✓ Skillet
- ✓ Slotted spoon

INGREDIENTS

- Semolina flour: 2 cups (480g)
- Ricotta cheese: 1 cup (250g)
- Saffron threads: a pinch
- Hot water: 1/4 cup (60ml), for saffron
- Salt: 1/2 tsp (2.5g)
- Large egg: 1
- Grated Pecorino cheese: 1/4 cup (60g)
- Unsalted butter: 2 tbsp (30g)
- Fresh mint leaves: for garnish

INSTRUCTIONS

Step 1 | Steep Saffron
Steep the saffron threads in hot water (1/4 cup or 60ml) for 10 minutes.

Step 2 | Prepare Dough
In a large bowl, mix semolina flour (2 cups or 480g) and salt (1/2 tsp or 2.5g). Add ricotta (1 cup or 250g), egg, and saffron water, mixing to form a dough. Add more flour if too sticky.

Step 3 | Shape Dumplings
Knead dough for 5 minutes, then divide and roll into ropes. Cut into pieces and press with a fork to form ridges.

Step 4 | Boil Dumplings
Cook dumplings in boiling salted water until they float, then cook for another minute. Remove with a slotted spoon.

Step 5 | Sauté
Melt butter (2 tbsp or 30g) in a skillet, add dumplings, and toss until golden. Sprinkle with Pecorino (1/4 cup or 60g) and melt.

Step 6 | Serve
Garnish with fresh mint and serve hot

NOTES

- **Dough Resting**: Let the dough rest for 30 minutes for easier handling.
- **Make Ahead**: Freeze uncooked dumplings and boil directly from frozen, adjusting cooking time as needed

PASTA

6 | BROCCOLI AND SAUSAGE PENNE (PENNE ALLA ROMANESCA), ITALY

INGREDIENTS

- Penne pasta: 12 oz (340g)
- Olive oil: 1 tbsp (15ml)
- Italian sausage, casings removed: 1 lb (454g)
- Romanesco broccoli, cut into florets: 1 large head (~4 cups or 300g)
- Garlic, minced: 4 cloves
- Chicken broth: 1/2 cup (120ml)
- Heavy cream: 1 cup (240ml)
- Grated Parmesan cheese: 1/2 cup (60g), plus extra for garnish
- Salt and pepper: to taste
- Red pepper flakes: optional, for a spicy kick

METHOD: POT
TIME: 45 MINUTE
SERVING: 4 PERSON
CALORIES: 750

This dish brings the streets of Rome to your table with Penne alla Romanesca. This pasta dish beautifully combines al dente penne, savory Italian sausage, and distinctively nutty Romanesco broccoli, all enveloped in a creamy, lightly seasoned sauce garnished with Parmesan.

- ✓ Large pot
- ✓ Large skillet
- ✓ Slotted spoon
- ✓ Measuring cups and spoons
- ✓ Knife and cutting board

INSTRUCTIONS

Step 1 | Boil Pasta
Cook penne in boiling salted water (12 oz or 340g) till al dente. Drain and set aside.

Step 2 | Brown Sausage
In skillet, heat olive oil (1 tbsp or 15ml), add sausage (1 lb or 454g), breaking into pieces, until browned.

Step 3 | Cook Romanesco
Remove sausage, add Romanesco (4 cups or 300g), cook until tender.

Step 4 | Add Garlic
Include minced garlic, sauté until fragrant.

Step 5 | Deglaze
Pour in chicken broth (1/2 cup or 120ml), simmer to reduce slightly.

Step 6 | Cream Sauce
Add heavy cream (1 cup or 240ml), simmer until thick.

Step 7 | Combine
Return sausage to skillet, add cooked pasta, season with salt, pepper, and chili flakes if using. Mix well.

Step 8 | Finish with Cheese
Off heat, add Parmesan (1/2 cup or 60g), stir until melted.

Step 9 | Serve
Garnish with more Parmesan.

NOTES

- **Lighter Version:** Substitute heavy cream with half-and-half or milk.
- **Vegetable Variants:** Use broccoli or cauliflower instead of Romanesco.
- **Storage:** Refrigerate and reheat within 2 days.

PASTA

7 ZUCCHINI LASAGNA WITH TURKEY AND PESTO, ITALY

A light, low-carb alternative to traditional pasta dish lasagna, this dish layers thinly sliced zucchini with lean turkey and homemade pesto, creating a nutritious and satisfying meal perfect for any dinner occasion.

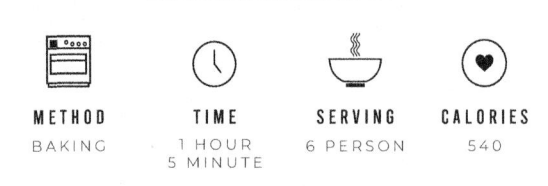

METHOD — BAKING
TIME — 1 HOUR 5 MINUTE
SERVING — 6 PERSON
CALORIES — 540

- 9x13 inch baking dish
- Mandoline or sharp knife
- Medium mixing bowl
- Large skillet
- Measuring cups and spoons
- Aluminum foil

INGREDIENTS

— Zucchini: 4 medium zucchini, sliced lengthwise (into thin strips)

— Turkey Mixture:
- tbsp olive oil
- 1 lb ground turkey
- 1 tsp salt
- 1/2 tsp black pepper

— Cheese Mixture:
- 1 cup part-skim ricotta cheese
- large egg
- 1/4 cup grated Parmesan cheese

— Other Ingredients:
- 2 cups homemade or store-bought pesto
- 2 cups shredded mozzarella cheese

INSTRUCTIONS

Step 1 | Prepare Oven and Dish
Preheat oven to 375°F (190°C). Grease a 9x13 inch baking dish with olive oil.

Step 2 | Cook Turkey
In a large skillet, heat olive oil over medium-high. Add ground turkey seasoned with salt and pepper. Cook until browned (5-7 mins). Set aside.

Step 3 | Prepare Zucchini
Slice zucchini using a mandoline into 1/8 inch thick strips. Salt and set aside on paper towels to draw out moisture (10 mins). Pat dry.

Step 4 | Mix Cheese
Combine ricotta, egg, and Parmesan in a mixing bowl.

Step 5 | Layer Lasagna
Start with a pesto layer in the dish, followed by zucchini strips. Add half the ricotta mixture, then half the turkey, and a cup of mozzarella. Repeat layers, ending with pesto.

Step 6 | Bake
Cover with foil and bake for 30 mins. Remove foil and bake for 15 more mins until top is golden.

Step 7 | Rest and Serve
Let lasagna sit for 10 mins before serving.

NOTES

- **Moisture Control:** Ensure zucchini is well-dried to prevent a watery lasagna.

- **Make Ahead:** Assemble the lasagna a day in advance and refrigerate. Adjust baking time if starting cold.

- **Vegetarian Option:** Replace turkey with plant-based crumbles or additional vegetables like mushrooms or bell peppers.

POULTRY

POULTRY

SHEET-PAN CHICKEN THIGHS WITH BRUSSELS SPROUTS & GNOCCHI, ITALY

METHOD OVEN | **TIME** 40 MINUTE | **SERVING** 4 PERSON | **CALORIES** 600

This one-pan wonder blends savory chicken, tender gnocchi, and crisp Brussels sprouts, seasoned with a mix of garlic, oregano, and a hint of red-wine vinegar. Perfect for an easy, flavorful weeknight dinner.

- ✓ Large rimmed baking sheet
- ✓ Large bowl
- ✓ Spoon or spatula

INGREDIENTS

- 4 tablespoons extra-virgin olive oil (2 fl oz or 60 ml)
- 2 tablespoons chopped fresh oregano (0.2 oz or 6g)
- 2 large cloves garlic, minced (approx. 0.2 oz or 6g)
- ½ teaspoon ground pepper (0.05 oz or 1.5g)
- ¼ teaspoon salt (0.15g)
- 1 pound Brussels sprouts, trimmed and quartered (16 oz or 453g)
- 1 package shelf-stable gnocchi (16 oz or 453g)
- 1 cup sliced red onion (4.2 oz or 120g)
- 4 boneless, skinless chicken thighs, trimmed (approx. 16 oz or 453g)
- 1 cup halved cherry tomatoes (5.3 oz or 150g)
- 1 tablespoon red-wine vinegar (0.5 fl oz or 15 ml)

INSTRUCTIONS

Step 1 | Preheat the Oven
Preheat your oven to 450 degrees F (220 degrees C).

Step 2 | Prepare Vegetables and Gnocchi
Combine 2 tablespoons (1 fl oz or 30 ml) olive oil, 1 tablespoon (0.1 oz or 3g) oregano, half the garlic, 1/4 teaspoon pepper, and 1/8 teaspoon salt in a large bowl. Add the Brussels sprouts (16 oz or 453g), gnocchi (16 oz or 453g), and onion (4.2 oz or 120g); toss to coat. Spread evenly on a large rimmed baking sheet.

Step 3 | Season the Chicken
In the same bowl, mix 1 tablespoon (0.5 fl oz or 15 ml) olive oil, the remaining 1 tablespoon oregano, remaining garlic, and the remaining 1/4 teaspoon pepper and 1/8 teaspoon salt. Add the chicken (approx. 16 oz or 453g) and toss to coat. Nestle the chicken among the vegetables on the baking sheet. Roast for 10 minutes.

Step 4 | Add Tomatoes and Continue Roasting
Remove the baking sheet from the oven, add the cherry tomatoes (5.3 oz or 150g), and stir to combine. Continue roasting until the Brussels sprouts are tender and the chicken is cooked through, about 10 more minutes.

Step 5 | Final Touches
Stir in the red-wine vinegar (0.5 fl oz or 15 ml) and the remaining 1 tablespoon olive oil (0.5 fl oz or 15 ml) into the vegetable mixture.

NOTES

- This dish is as versatile as it is delicious. Feel free to experiment with other vegetables or herbs to tailor it to your taste preferences.

POULTRY

2 SUN-DRIED TOMATO CHICKEN, ITALY

INGREDIENTS

- 1 ½ pounds chicken breasts (24 oz or 680g)
- 1 tablespoon Italian Seasoning
- 1 ¼ teaspoons kosher salt
- 2 tablespoons extra virgin olive oil (1 fl oz or 30 ml)
- 3 ounces sun-dried tomatoes, sliced (3 oz or 85g)
- 1 small yellow onion, thinly sliced (approximately 4 oz or 113g)
- 4 large garlic cloves, minced (approximately 0.8 oz or 23g)
- ⅓ cup white wine (2.7 fl oz or 80 ml)
- 1 ¾ cup whole milk (14 fl oz or 414 ml)
- 1 ½ tablespoons corn starch
- 2 cups baby spinach (approximately 2 oz or 57g)
- ¼ cup sliced Kalamata olives (approximately 1.5 oz or 43g)

METHOD: SKILLET
TIME: 30 MINUTE
SERVING: 6 PERSON
CALORIES: 311

Sun-Dried Tomato Chicken recipe delivers an enticing blend of flavors, featuring a creamy sauce filled with spinach, olives, and sun-dried tomatoes—all without using heavy cream. It's a quick and delicious choice for a satisfying weeknight dinner that comes together in just 30 minutes.

- ✓ Cutting board
- ✓ Large skillet
- ✓ Sharp knife
- ✓ Wooden spoon or spatula
- ✓ Small bowl

INSTRUCTIONS

Step 1 | Prepare the Chicken Cutlets
Halve the chicken breasts (24 oz or 680g total) horizontally to create thin cutlets. Season with Italian seasoning and ¾ teaspoon of the kosher salt.

Step 2 | Heat the Skillet
Warm the olive oil (1 fl oz or 30 ml) in a large skillet over medium-high heat. Cook the chicken cutlets for 4 to 6 minutes on each side until they reach an internal temperature of 165°F. Remove and set aside.

Step 3 | Make the Sauce
In the same skillet, add sun-dried tomatoes (3 oz or 85g), onion (4 oz or 113g), and garlic (0.8 oz or 23g), along with white wine (2.7 fl oz or 80 ml) and the remaining ½ teaspoon salt. Cook until the onions soften, about 2 to 3 minutes, scraping the skillet to lift the fond.

Step 4 | Thicken the Sauce
Combine corn starch with 3 tablespoons of cold water in a small bowl. Add milk (14 fl oz or 414 ml) to the skillet and bring to a simmer. Stir in the corn starch mixture until the sauce thickens.

Step 5 | Final Touches
Reduce heat to low, stir in spinach (2 oz or 57g) and olives (1.5 oz or 43g). Slice the chicken and return it to the skillet to warm. Adjust seasoning as needed.

NOTES

- Serve this delightful chicken and sauce over a bed of pasta or with crusty bread to soak up the flavorful sauce. It's a hearty and nutritious dish that's sure to please any palate.

POULTRY

3 CHICKEN SOUVLAKI WITH OREGANO AND GARLIC, GREECE

Experience the vibrant flavors of Greece with this Greek Chicken Souvlaki recipe. Marinated in oregano, garlic, and Mediterranean spices, these grilled skewers are perfect for a quick dinner or a flavorful appetizer.

METHOD GRILL
TIME 25 MINUTE
SERVING 4 PERSON
CALORIES 310

- ✓ Whisk
- ✓ Mixing bowl
- ✓ Grill
- ✓ Skewers

INGREDIENTS

- 1 1/2 pounds boneless, skinless chicken breast, cut into 1-inch cubes (24 oz or 680g)
- 1/4 cup olive oil (2 fl oz or 60 ml)
- Juice of 1 lemon (about 2 tbsp)
- 3 cloves garlic, minced (approx. 0.3 oz or 9g)
- 2 tbsp fresh oregano, chopped, or 1 tbsp dried (0.2 oz or 5g fresh)
- 1 tsp paprika (0.1 oz or 2g)
- 1/2 tsp crushed red pepper flakes (optional) (0.05 oz or 1.5g)
- Salt and pepper to taste

INSTRUCTIONS

Step 1 | Prepare the Marinade
Whisk olive oil (2 fl oz or 60 ml), lemon juice (2 tbsp), garlic (0.3 oz or 9g), oregano (0.2 oz or 5g fresh), paprika (0.1 oz or 2g), optional red pepper flakes (0.05 oz or 1.5g), and a pinch of salt and pepper in a bowl.

Step 2 | Marinate the Chicken
Add chicken (24 oz or 680g) to the marinade, mix well, cover, and chill for 30 minutes to 2 hours.

Step 3 | Prepare the Skewers
If using wooden skewers, soak them in water for 20 minutes to prevent burning.

Step 4 | Grill the Chicken
Preheat the grill to medium-high. Thread chicken onto skewers, leaving space between pieces. Grill for 10-12 minutes, turning occasionally, until cooked through and slightly charred.

Step 5 | Rest and Serve
Let rest for a few minutes before serving.

NOTES

- Serve with tzatziki sauce, fresh lemon juice, and warm pita for a complete Greek meal. Store leftovers for up to 3 days. Adjust lemon juice to suit your taste. Ensure chicken reaches an internal temperature of 165°F (75°C).

POULTRY

4 CHICKEN STIFADO WITH ONIONS AND CINNAMON, GREECE

METHOD
POT

TIME
1 HOUR 20 MINUTE

SERVING
4 PERSON

CALORIES
450

The Chicken Stifado, is a savory stew that marries tender chicken thighs with a rich, cinnamon-spiced tomato sauce. This comforting dish showcases a delicious interplay of flavors and is perfect for a hearty meal.

- Large pot or Dutch oven
- Measuring cups and spoons
- Knife and chopping board

INGREDIENTS

- 2.5 lbs chicken thighs, bone-in and skin-on (about 40 oz or 1135g)
- 2 tbsp olive oil (30 ml)
- 2 large onions, thinly sliced
- 4 garlic cloves, minced
- 1 tsp ground cinnamon
- 1/4 tsp ground cloves
- 1/2 tsp ground allspice
- 1 bay leaf
- 14 oz canned diced tomatoes (400g)
- 1/4 cup red wine vinegar (60 ml)
- 1/2 cup red wine (120 ml)
- Salt and pepper to taste
- Fresh parsley, chopped (for garnish)

INSTRUCTIONS

Step 1 | Brown the Chicken
Heat olive oil (30 ml) in a large pot over medium-high heat. Season chicken thighs with salt and pepper, then brown on both sides. Remove and set aside.

Step 2 | Caramelize the Onions
Reduce heat to medium. Add onions to the pot and caramelize, about 10 minutes.

Step 3 | Add Garlic and Spices
Stir in garlic (4 cloves), cinnamon (1 tsp), cloves (1/4 tsp), allspice (1/2 tsp), and bay leaf. Cook until fragrant, about 1 minute.

Step 4 | Add Liquids and Tomatoes
Add diced tomatoes (14 oz or 400g), red wine vinegar (60 ml), and red wine (120 ml). Bring to a simmer.

Step 5 | Simmer the Stew
Return chicken to the pot, cover, and simmer for 45 minutes until chicken is tender.

Step 6 | Final Touches
Remove bay leaf, adjust seasoning with salt and pepper, and garnish with parsley before serving.

NOTES

- Add tomato paste for a thicker sauce.
- For authenticity, mix in shallots with the onions.
- Substitute with boneless chicken thighs if preferred, adjusting cooking time.

POULTRY

5 ROASTED CHICKEN WITH PRUNES AND CINNAMON, TURKEY

INGREDIENTS

- 1 whole chicken (4-5 lbs or 1.8-2.3 kg)
- 1 cup prunes (150 g)
- 2 cinnamon sticks
- 1 tbsp ground cinnamon (15 g)
- 2 tbsp olive oil (30 ml)
- 1 tsp salt (5 g)
- 1/2 tsp black pepper (2 g)
- 4 cloves garlic, minced (12 g)
- 1 large onion, sliced (200 g)
- 1/2 cup chicken broth (120 ml)
- 1 tbsp honey (21 g)
- Fresh herbs (thyme or rosemary), for garnish

METHOD OVEN | **TIME** 1 HOUR 50 MINUTES | **SERVING** 4 PERSON | **CALORIES** 690

Travel to Bursa with this exquisite roasted chicken, enhanced with the sweetness of prunes and the warm spice of cinnamon. This dish combines deep, comforting flavors with a succulent texture, offering a delightful taste of Turkish cuisine.

- ✓ Roasting pan
- ✓ Small bowl
- ✓ Meat thermometer
- ✓ Basting brush

INSTRUCTIONS

Step 1 | Preheat the Oven
Preheat the oven to 375°F (190°C). Rinse and dry the chicken, then place it in a roasting pan.

Step 2 | Season the Chicken
Mix ground cinnamon (15 g), salt (5 g), and black pepper (2 g) in a small bowl. Rub the mixture all over the chicken, under the skin, and inside the cavity.

Step 3 | Stuff the Chicken
Stuff the chicken cavity with prunes (150 g) and cinnamon sticks.

Step 4 | Prepare the Roasting Pan
Drizzle olive oil (30 ml) over the chicken and rub it into the skin. Scatter onions (200 g) and garlic (12 g) around the chicken in the pan.

Step 5 | Add Broth
Pour chicken broth (120 ml) into the pan, avoiding the chicken to preserve the spice rub.

Step 6 | Roast the Chicken
Roast for approximately 1 hour and 30 minutes, or until the internal temperature reaches 165°F (75°C), basting occasionally.

Step 7 | Glaze the Chicken
In the last 10 minutes of roasting, brush the chicken with honey (21 g) for a caramelized glaze.

Step 8 | Rest and Serve
Let the chicken rest for 10 minutes after roasting before carving. Garnish with fresh herbs.

NOTES

- The combination of prunes and cinnamon provides a distinctively sweet and spicy flavor, typical of Bursa's regional cuisine.

- Resting the chicken ensures it retains its juices, enhancing flavor and tenderness.

- Serve with roasted vegetables or a Mediterranean salad to round out the meal.

POULTRY

6 CHICKEN GYROS WITH PITA BREAD & TZATZIKI SAUCE, GREECE

Greek Chicken Gyros are a delightful meal that combines tender grilled chicken with creamy tzatziki sauce, wrapped in soft pita bread. This quick and flavorful dish is perfect for any day of the week.

METHOD GRILL
TIME 25 MINUTE
SERVING 4 PERSON
CALORIES 400

- Grill or grilling pan
- Cutting board
- Mixing bowl
- Knife
- Measuring cups and spoons

INGREDIENTS

- 4 chicken breasts, thinly sliced (about 2 lbs or 900g)
- 2 tbsp olive oil (1 fl oz or 30 ml)
- 2 tbsp Greek seasoning (or a mix of oregano, thyme, and garlic powder) (10g)
- 1 cup tzatziki sauce (recipe in the sauce & spices chapter) (8 oz or 227g)
- 4 pita breads
- 1 tomato, sliced (about 6 oz or 170g)
- 1 onion, sliced (about 4 oz or 113g)
- Salt and pepper to taste

INSTRUCTIONS

Step 1 | Prepare the Chicken
In a mixing bowl, combine the chicken breasts (2 lbs or 900g) with olive oil (2 tbsp or 30 ml), Greek seasoning (10g), salt, and pepper. Ensure each piece is evenly coated.

Step 2 | Grill the Chicken
Preheat your grill or grilling pan to medium-high heat. Grill the chicken slices for about 10-12 minutes, turning occasionally, until they are fully cooked and have nice char marks.

Step 3 | Warm the Pita Breads
Warm the pita breads briefly on the grill.

Step 4 | Assemble the Gyros
Lay each pita flat and add a layer of grilled chicken, tzatziki sauce (8 oz or 227g), sliced tomatoes (6 oz or 170g), and onions (4 oz or 113g).

Step 5 | Serve
Fold the pitas over the fillings and serve immediately.

NOTES

- Tzatziki sauce adds a creamy, tangy element to the gyros.

- This dish pairs well with a side of Greek salad or seasoned fries.

- This dish pairs well with a side of Greek salad or seasoned fries.

POULTRY

7 CHICKEN WITH RICE, SPAIN

METHOD SIMMER | **TIME** 30 MINUTE | **SERVING** 4 PERSON | **CALORIES** 500

Spanish Chicken and Rice, also known as Arroz con Pollo, combines juicy chicken thighs with aromatic rice infused with saffron and traditional Spanish spices. This hearty one-pot meal is beloved for its simplicity and rich flavors.

- ✓ Large skillet or Dutch oven
- ✓ Measuring cups and spoons
- ✓ Knife
- ✓ Measuring cups and spoons

INGREDIENTS

- 4 chicken thighs, bone-in and skin-on (about 2 lbs or 900g)
- 1 cup rice (about 6.5 oz or 185g)
- 2 cups chicken broth (16 fl oz or 475 ml)
- 1 onion, chopped (about 4 oz or 113g)
- 1 bell pepper, chopped (about 6 oz or 170g)
- 2 cloves garlic, minced (about 1 tbsp or 15 ml)
- 1 tsp paprika (5 ml)
- 1/2 tsp saffron threads (optional for authentic flavor) (about 0.1g)
- 2 tbsp olive oil (1 fl oz or 30 ml)
- Salt and pepper to taste

INSTRUCTIONS

Step 1 | Prepare the Chicken
Season the chicken thighs (2 lbs or 900g) with salt and pepper.

Step 2 | Cook the Chicken
In a large skillet or Dutch oven, heat olive oil (2 tbsp or 30 ml) over medium heat. Add the seasoned chicken thighs and brown them on both sides, about 3-4 minutes per side. Remove from the pan and set aside.

Step 3 | Sauté Vegetables
In the same pan, add the chopped onion (4 oz or 113g) and bell pepper (6 oz or 170g). Cook until soft, about 5 minutes. Add minced garlic (1 tbsp or 15 ml) and cook for an additional minute until fragrant.

Step 4 | Combine and Cook
Stir in paprika (1 tsp or 5 ml) and saffron threads (0.1g), then add rice (1 cup or 185g) and chicken broth (2 cups or 475 ml). Bring to a boil. Return the chicken to the skillet, reduce heat to low, cover, and simmer for 20 minutes, or until the rice is tender and the chicken is cooked through.

Step 5 | Serve Fluff the rice with a fork and adjust seasoning with additional salt and pepper if needed. Serve hot.

NOTES

- Saffron adds a characteristic color and flavor to the dish but can be omitted if not available.
- This dish pairs well with a simple green salad or steamed vegetables for a complete meal.

PULSES

PULSES

1 BAKED BEANS WITH TOMATOES AND DILL, GREECE

INGREDIENTS

- Dried navy beans, soaked overnight: 1 lb (450 g)
- Olive oil: 2 tbsp (30 ml)
- Large onion, finely chopped: 1
- Garlic cloves, minced: 4
- Canned diced tomatoes: 1 can (14 oz or 400 g)
- Tomato paste: 2 tbsp (30 g)
- Granulated sugar: 1 tsp (4 g)
- Salt: 1 ½ tsp (9 g)
- Freshly ground black pepper: ½ tsp (2.5 g)
- Red wine vinegar: 2 tbsp (30 ml)
- Water: 1 ½ cups (360 ml)
- Fresh dill, chopped, plus extra for garnish: ¼ cup (15 g)

METHOD OVEN
TIME 1 HOUR 45 MINUTE
SERVING 6 PERSON
CALORIES 250

Savor the heartiness of Greek cuisine with this rustic and flavorsome dish of baked beans, simmered in a rich tomato sauce and infused with the freshness of dill. This Greek Style Baked Beans with Tomatoes and Dill recipe brings a touch of the Mediterranean to your table, perfect as a comforting dinner or a substantial mezze option.

✓ Ovenproof pot with lid
✓ Large pot for boiling beans
✓ Colander for draining beans
✓ Knife and chopping board
✓ Measuring cups and spoons

INSTRUCTIONS

Step 1 | Preheat Oven
Preheat your oven to 350°F (175°C).

Step 2 | Cook Beans
Drain and rinse the soaked navy beans (1 lb or 450 g). Place them in a large pot, cover with water, and bring to a boil. Reduce heat and simmer for 30 minutes or until beans are just tender. Drain and set aside.

Step 3 | Prepare Base
In a large ovenproof pot, heat olive oil (2 tbsp or 30 ml) over medium heat. Add the chopped onion (1) and cook until translucent, about 5 minutes. Stir in the minced garlic (4 cloves) and cook for another minute.

Step 4 | Combine Ingredients
Add the canned diced tomatoes (14 oz or 400 g), tomato paste (2 tbsp or 30 g), granulated sugar (1 tsp or 4 g), salt (1 ½ tsp or 9 g), black pepper (½ tsp or 2.5 g), and red wine vinegar (2 tbsp or 30 ml) to the pot. Stir to combine.

Step 5 | Simmer Beans
Add the pre-cooked beans and water (1 ½ cups or 360 ml) to the pot and bring the mixture to a simmer.

Step 6 | Bake
Cover the pot with a lid or aluminum foil and transfer it to the preheated oven. Bake for 1 hour, or until the beans are soft and the sauce has thickened.

Step 7 | Add Dill
Remove from the oven, stir in the chopped dill (¼ cup or 15 g), and adjust seasoning if necessary.

Step 8 | Serve
Let the baked beans rest for 10 minutes before serving. Garnish with additional fresh dill.

NOTES

- For an even richer flavor, consider adding a bay leaf or two during the baking process.
- If you prefer a more traditional Greek experience, try using gigantes beans instead of navy beans.
- As a time-saving tip, canned beans can be used in place of dried beans to cut down on prep time; just be sure to rinse them thoroughly before use.

PULSES

2 | LENTILS WITH RICE AND CARAMELIZED ONIONS (MUJADDARA), CYPRUS

Mujaddara, a cherished dish from the heart of Cyprus, steeped in history and tradition. This beloved meal, dating back to medieval times, expertly blends earthy lentils and fragrant rice with deeply caramelized onions. Celebrated for its hearty, nutritious qualities, Mujaddara is a timeless comfort food perfect for any day.

METHOD — STOVETOP
TIME — 1 HOUR
SERVING — 4 PERSON
CALORIES — 350

- ✓ Large pan
- ✓ Wooden spoon
- ✓ Measuring cups and spoons
- ✓ Chopping board
- ✓ Knife

INGREDIENTS

- Brown or Green Lentils: 1 cup (190 g / 6.7 oz)
- Long-Grain Rice: 1 cup (185 g / 6.5 oz)
- Onions: 3 large, thinly sliced (450 g / 1 lb)
- Olive Oil: 3 tbsp (45 ml)
- Cumin Seeds: 2 tsp (4 g)
- Ground Cinnamon: ½ tsp (1 g)
- Vegetable Broth: 4 cups (960 ml)
- Salt and Pepper: to taste
- Fresh Parsley: chopped, for garnish (optional)

INSTRUCTIONS

Step 1 | Rinse Lentils
Rinse 1 cup lentils (190 g) under cold water until clear. Drain and set aside.

Step 2 | Caramelize Onions
In a large pan, heat 2 tbsp olive oil (30 ml). Add 2 tsp cumin seeds (4 g). Add sliced onions (450 g), cook until golden then reduce heat, and caramelize for about 30-35 minutes.

Step 3 | Combine Ingredients
Remove half the onions for garnish. To remaining onions, add drained lentils, 1 cup rice (185 g), ½ tsp cinnamon (1 g), salt, and pepper. Mix well.

Step 4 | Cook Mujaddara
Add 4 cups vegetable broth (960 ml), bring to boil. Reduce heat, simmer covered until lentils and rice are tender, about 20 minutes.

Step 5 | Rest and Serve
Remove from heat, cover for 5 more minutes, fluff with fork. Serve garnished with caramelized onions and chopped parsley.

NOTES

- **Gluten-Free:** Ensure broth is gluten-free.
- **Meal Prep:** Stores well in the fridge for up to 3 days. Flavors enhance overnight.
- **Vegan Option:** Use vegan broth.

PULSES

3 WHITE BEAN SALAD WITH TOMATOES AND PARSLEY (PIYAZ), TURKEY

METHOD
NO-COOK

TIME
15 MINUTE

SERVING
4 PERSON

CALORIES
200

This Turkish White Bean Salad, known as Piyaz, is a refreshing blend of creamy beans, juicy tomatoes, sharp onions, and vibrant parsley, all brought together with a tangy lemon and olive oil dressing. Perfect as a light lunch or a flavorful side dish.

- ✓ Large mixing bowl
- ✓ Small whisk or fork
- ✓ Knife
- ✓ Cutting board

INGREDIENTS

- 1 can white beans (15 oz or 425 g), drained and rinsed
- 2 medium tomatoes (about 10 oz or 300 g), **diced**
- 1 medium red onion (about 5 oz or 150 g), **thinly sliced**
- 1 cup parsley (60 g), **finely chopped**
- 2 tbsp olive oil (1 fl oz or 30 ml)
- 2 tbsp lemon juice (1 fl oz or 30 ml)
- 1 tsp sea salt (5 g)
- 1/2 tsp freshly ground black pepper
- 1 tsp sumac, optional, for garnish
- 1 hard-boiled egg, sliced, optional, for garnish

INSTRUCTIONS

Step 1 | Prepare the Beans and Vegetables
Drain and rinse the canned white beans (15 oz or 425 g) and place them in a large mixing bowl.
Dice the tomatoes (10 oz or 300 g) into small, bite-sized pieces and thinly slice the red onion (5 oz or 150 g). Add both to the bowl with the beans.

Step 2 | Chop the Parsley
Finely chop the parsley (60 g), discarding any thick stems. Add the chopped parsley to the mixing bowl with the other ingredients.

Step 3 | Make the Dressing
In a small bowl, whisk together the olive oil (1 fl oz or 30 ml), lemon juice (1 fl oz or 30 ml), sea salt (5 g), and black pepper (0.025 oz or 0.75 g) until well combined.

Step 4 | Combine Ingredients
Pour the dressing over the bean and vegetable mixture. Gently toss everything together, ensuring that the dressing coats all ingredients evenly.

Step 5 | Garnish and Serve
If you're using sumac (1 tsp), sprinkle it over the salad for an added zest, and if desired, garnish with slices of hard-boiled egg.
Allow the salad to sit for about 10 minutes before serving to let the flavors meld together. Serve as a refreshing mezze or a light lunch.

NOTES

- For best flavor, use high-quality olive oil and fresh lemon juice

- The salad can be refrigerated for up to 2 days, but it's best enjoyed fresh.

- If you prefer, you can use dry white beans. Simply soak overnight and boil until tender before using them in the recipe.

PULSES

4 RIBOLLITA WITH KALE AND CRISPY PANCETTA, ITALY

INGREDIENTS

- 4 ounces pancetta, diced (about 113g)
- 2 tbsp olive oil (1 fl oz or 30ml)
- 1 large onion, chopped (about 1 cup or 150g)
- 2 carrots, peeled and diced (about 1 cup or 130g)
- 2 celery stalks, diced (about 1 cup or 100g)
- 4 garlic cloves, minced (about 0.5 oz or 15g)
- 1 tsp dried thyme (about 1g)
- 1/2 tsp red pepper flakes (about 0.5g)
- 1 can diced tomatoes (14 oz or 400g)
- 1 can cannellini beans, drained and rinsed (15 oz or 425g)
- 4 cups low-sodium vegetable broth (32 fl oz or 950ml)
- 4 cups chopped kale, stems removed (about 7 oz or 200g)
- Salt and pepper to taste
- 1 loaf crusty Italian bread, stale and torn into pieces
- Grated Parmesan cheese for serving

METHOD: POT
TIME: 1 HOUR 15 MINUTES
SERVING: 6 PERSON
CALORIES: 320

Revel in the rustic charm of Italian Ribollita with Kale and Crispy Pancetta, a hearty and nutritious soup that epitomizes the essence of the Mediterranean diet. This Tuscan classic combines cannellini beans, kale, and a medley of vegetables in a thick broth, topped with savory crispy pancetta for a delightful crunch and flavor boost. Perfect for a cozy dinner, this Ribollita is a soul-warming dish that will become a staple in your culinary repertoire.

- ✓ Large pot
- ✓ Slotted spoon
- ✓ Chef's knife
- ✓ Cutting board
- ✓ Measuring cups and spoons

INSTRUCTIONS

Step 1 | Cook Pancetta
In a large pot, cook the diced pancetta (113g) over medium heat until crispy. Remove the pancetta with a slotted spoon and set aside on a paper towel to drain.

Step 2 | Sauté Vegetables
In the same pot, add olive oil (1 fl oz or 30ml), onion (150g), carrots (130g), and celery (100g). Cook over medium heat until the vegetables are softened, about 5 to 7 minutes.

Step 3 | Add Garlic and Spices
Add minced garlic (0.5 oz or 15g), dried thyme (1g), and red pepper flakes (0.5g). Cook for another minute until fragrant.

Step 4 | Add Tomatoes and Scrape Pot
Pour in the diced tomatoes (14 oz or 400g) with their juices, and scrape any browned bits off the bottom of the pot.

Step 5 | Add Beans and Broth
Stir in the cannellini beans (15 oz or 425g) and vegetable broth (32 fl oz or 950ml). Bring to a simmer.

Step 6 | Add Bread and Kale
Add the torn pieces of stale bread and chopped kale (7 oz or 200g) to the pot. Season with salt and pepper to taste

Step 7 | Simmer
Allow the soup to simmer for about 45 minutes, or until the bread is completely broken down and the soup has thickened. Stir occasionally, mashing some of the beans against the side of the pot to help thicken the soup.

Step 8 | Adjust Seasoning and Serve
Taste and adjust the seasoning as needed. Serve hot, topped with the crispy pancetta and a sprinkle of grated Parmesan cheese.

NOTES

- The soup is traditionally served the day after preparation when the flavors have melded together, hence the name "ribollita" which means "reboiled."

- For a vegetarian version, omit the pancetta and use a sprinkle of smoked paprika for a similar smoky flavor.

- Leftovers can be stored in the refrigerator for up to 3 days and taste even better as the flavors continue to develop.

PULSES

5 SAUERKRAUT AND BEAN STEW (JOTA), SLOVENIA

A hearty and savory stew that embodies the essence of Slovenian comfort food, this Slovenian Sauerkraut and Bean Stew, known as Jota, is a delightful blend of tangy sauerkraut, creamy beans, and smoky meat. It's a nourishing dish perfect for chilly evenings.

METHOD POT
TIME 1 HOUR 45 MINUTE
SERVING 6 PERSON
CALORIES 350

- Large pot
- Knife
- Cutting board
- Measuring spoons
- Measuring cups

INGREDIENTS

- 1 lb dried borlotti or cranberry beans, soaked overnight (about 450g)
- 1 lb sauerkraut, drained (about 450g)
- 6 cups water (about 1.4 liters)
- 1 large onion, diced (about 1 cup or 150g)
- 3 cloves garlic, minced (about 0.35 oz or 10g)
- 8 oz smoked pork or sausage, diced (about 225g)
- 2 bay leaves
- 1 tsp caraway seeds (about 1g)
- ½ tsp black pepper (about 1g)
- 2 tbsp olive oil (1 fl oz or 30ml)
- Salt to taste

NOTES

- For a vegetarian version, omit the smoked pork or sausage and add a drop of liquid smoke for that characteristic smoky flavor.
- If you prefer a thinner stew, adjust the amount of water to suit your taste.
- The stew tastes even better the next day as the flavors meld together overnight.
- This dish is traditionally served with a slice of crusty bread on the side.

INSTRUCTIONS

Step 1 | Cook the Beans
Begin by rinsing the pre-soaked beans. Place them in a large pot, cover with water, and bring to a boil. Reduce the heat to a simmer and cook for about 1 hour or until the beans are tender. Drain and set aside.

Step 2 | Sauté Onions and Meat
In the same pot, heat olive oil (1 fl oz or 30ml) over medium heat. Add the diced onion (1 cup or 150g) and sauté until translucent, around 5 minutes. Add the minced garlic (0.35 oz or 10g) and diced smoked pork or sausage (225g). Cook for an additional 5-7 minutes, or until the meat is slightly browned.

Step 3 | Add Sauerkraut and Beans
Stir in the drained sauerkraut (450g), cooked beans, bay leaves, caraway seeds (1g), and black pepper (1g). Pour in 6 cups of water (1.4 liters), or enough to cover the ingredients in the pot.

Step 4 | Simmer the Stew
Bring the stew to a boil, then reduce the heat to maintain a gentle simmer. Cover and let it cook for 30 minutes, stirring occasionally.

Step 5 | Thicken and Season
After 30 minutes, remove the lid and continue to simmer for another 15-20 minutes, or until the stew has thickened to your liking. Adjust the seasoning with salt, and remove the bay leaves before serving.

PULSES

6 | STUFFED EGGPLANT WITH LENTILS, WALNUTS, AND POMEGRANATE GLAZE, LEBANON

METHOD: OVEN
TIME: 1 HOUR
SERVING: 4 PERSON
CALORIES: 350

This savory and slightly sweet Stuffed Eggplant with Lentils, Walnuts, and Pomegranate Molasses is a hearty, plant-based dish that brings a burst of Mediterranean flavors to your dinner table.

- ✓ Medium saucepan
- ✓ Large skillet
- ✓ Baking shee
- ✓ Oven

INGREDIENTS

- 4 medium eggplants (about 2 lbs or 900g)
- 1 cup green lentils (7 oz or 200g), **rinsed and drained**
- 2 1/2 cups water (20 fl oz or 600ml) **for cooking lentils**
- 1 large onion (7 oz or 200g), **finely chopped**
- 3 cloves garlic, minced
- 1/2 cup walnuts (2 oz or 60g), **roughly chopped**
- 1/4 cup pomegranate glaze (2 fl oz or 60ml) (sauces chapter)
- 1 tsp ground cumin (about 2.5g)
- 1 tsp smoked paprika (about 2.5g)
- 1/2 tsp ground cinnamon (about 1.25g)
- 2 tbsp olive oil (1 fl oz or 30ml), **plus extra for brushing**
- 1/2 cup fresh parsley (0.5 oz or 15g), chopped
- Salt and pepper to taste
- Pomegranate seeds for garnish (optional)

NOTES

- The lentil stuffing can be prepared ahead of time and refrigerated for up to two days before stuffing the eggplants.
- Leftovers can be stored in an airtight container and refrigerated for up to three days. Reheat in the oven or microwave before serving.

INSTRUCTIONS

Step 1 | Preheat Oven and Prepare Eggplants
Preheat your oven to 400°F (200°C).
Cut the eggplants in half lengthwise and scoop out the flesh to create a hollow center, leaving about 1/2 inch of flesh on the skin. Brush the insides with olive oil and season with salt and pepper. Place on a baking sheet and bake for 25 minutes, or until the eggplants are tender.

Step 2 | Cook Lentils
While the eggplants are baking, bring 2 1/2 cups of water (20 fl oz or 600ml) to a boil in a medium saucepan. Add the lentils (7 oz or 200g) and a pinch of salt, reduce the heat to low, cover, and simmer for about 20 minutes or until the lentils are tender but not mushy. Drain any excess water.

Step 3 | Sauté Onions and Spices
In a large skillet, heat 2 tablespoons of olive oil (1 fl oz or 30ml) over medium heat. Add the onions (7 oz or 200g) and garlic, and sauté until translucent, about 5 minutes. Stir in the cumin (2.5g), smoked paprika (2.5g), and cinnamon (1.25g), and cook for another 2 minutes.

Step 4 | Combine Lentils and Walnuts
Add the cooked lentils and walnuts (2 oz or 60g) to the skillet, and cook for 5 minutes, stirring occasionally. Pour in the pomegranate glaze (2 fl oz or 60ml) and cook for an additional 2 minutes, allowing the flavors to meld. Remove the skillet from the heat and stir in the chopped parsley (15g). Adjust seasoning with salt and pepper to your taste.

Step 5 | Stuff and Bake Eggplants
Once the eggplants are tender, remove them from the oven and fill each one with the lentil and walnut mixture. Return to the oven and bake for an additional 15 minutes.

Step 6 | Serve
Serve the stuffed eggplants warm, drizzled with more pomegranate glaze and garnished with pomegranate seeds if desired.

PULSES

7 RED LENTIL AND QUINOA WITH CUMIN, NORTH AFRICA

INGREDIENTS

- 1 cup red lentils (200g)
- 1 cup quinoa (170g)
- 3 tablespoons extra virgin olive oil (44ml)
- 2 tablespoons fresh lemon juice (30ml)
- 1 teaspoon cumin (2g)
- 1 cup cherry tomatoes, halved (150g)
- 1 medium cucumber, diced (200g)
- 1 small red onion, finely chopped (70g)
- 1/2 cup fresh parsley, chopped (15g)
- 1/2 cup feta cheese, crumbled (75g)
- Salt and pepper to taste

METHOD MIXING | **TIME** 35 MINUTE | **SERVING** 4 PERSON | **CALORIES** 350

An invigorating blend of protein-rich red lentils and quinoa, this Mediterranean Red Lentil and Quinoa Salad with Cumin is a nutritious dish that bursts with vibrant flavors and a variety of textures. Perfect for a wholesome lunch or a hearty side, this salad is both healthful and satisfying.

- ✓ Large bowl
- ✓ Whisk
- ✓ Knife
- ✓ Cutting board
- ✓ Medium saucepan
- ✓ Colander
- ✓ Measuring cups and spoons

INSTRUCTIONS

Step 1 | Cook the Lentils
Rinse the red lentils under cold running water until the water runs clear.
In a medium saucepan, combine the red lentils with 2 cups (473ml) of water. Bring to a boil, then reduce heat and simmer for 10-15 minutes or until lentils are tender but not mushy. Drain any excess water and let cool.

Step 2 | Cook the Quinoa
Meanwhile, rinse the quinoa under cold running water until the water runs clear.
In another medium saucepan, combine the quinoa with 2 cups (473ml) of water. Bring to a boil, reduce the heat to low, cover, and simmer for 15 minutes or until the water is absorbed and the quinoa is fluffy. Remove from heat and let stand covered for 5 minutes. Fluff with a fork and let cool.

Step 3 | Prepare the Dressing
In a large bowl, whisk together the olive oil (44ml), fresh lemon juice (30ml), cumin (2g), salt, and pepper to create the dressing.

Step 4 | Assemble the Salad
Add the cooled lentils and quinoa to the dressing and toss to coat evenly.
Stir in the cherry tomatoes (150g), cucumber (200g), red onion (70g), and fresh parsley (15g). Mix until well combined.
Gently fold in the crumbled feta cheese (75g).

Step 5 | Adjust Seasoning and Serve
Taste and adjust seasoning if necessary. Serve chilled or at room temperature.

NOTES

- To make this dish vegan, simply omit the feta cheese or replace it with a vegan cheese alternative.
- For the best flavor, allow the salad to marinate in the refrigerator for at least 30 minutes before serving.

SALADS & MEZZES

SALADS & MEZZES

1. BULGUR WHEAT SALAD WITH TOMATOES AND CUCUMBERS (KISIR), TURKEY

Kısır is a cherished staple in Turkish cuisine, particularly popular in the south-eastern regions. This dish dates back to ancient Anatolia's agricultural practices, where bulgur was prized for its nutritional value and longevity. Kısır is perfect as a light lunch or as part of a mezze spread.

METHOD MIXING | **TIME** 30 MINUTE | **SERVING** 4 PERSON | **CALORIES** 250

- ✓ Whisk
- ✓ Small bowl
- ✓ Large mixing bowl
- ✓ Fork
- ✓ Knife
- ✓ Cutting board

INGREDIENTS

- 1 cup Bulgur wheat (180g)
- 1 1/4 cups Boiling water (300ml)
- 2 Medium tomatoes, finely diced (about 1 cup/180g)
- 1 Medium cucumber, finely diced (about 3/4 cup/100g)
- 3 Green onions, thinly sliced (about 1/3 cup/50g)
- 1 cup Fresh parsley, finely chopped (60g)
- 1/4 cup Fresh mint, finely chopped (15g)
- 1/4 cup Olive oil (60ml)
- 3 tbsp Lemon juice (45ml)
- 1 tbsp Pomegranate glaze (Spices & Sauces chapter) (15ml)
- 1 tbsp Tomato paste (15g)
- 1 tsp Ground cumin (2g)
- 1 tsp Paprika (2g)
- 1/2 tsp Salt (3g)
- 1/4 tsp Black pepper (0.5g)
- 1/2 tsp Crushed red pepper flakes (optional, 1g)

INSTRUCTIONS

Step 1 | Prepare the bulgur
In a large mixing bowl, add bulgur wheat (180g). Cover with boiling water (1 1/4 cups or 300ml). Cover the bowl and let sit for 10-15 minutes until water is absorbed and bulgur is tender.

Step 2 | Fluff and cool the bulgur
Once tender, fluff the bulgur with a fork to separate the grains. Allow to cool to room temperature.

Step 3 | Make the dressing
In a small bowl, whisk together olive oil (1/4 cup or 60ml), lemon juice (3 tbsp or 45ml), pomegranate molasses (1 tbsp or 15ml), tomato paste (1 tbsp or 15g), cumin (1 tsp or 2g), paprika (1 tsp or 2g), salt (1/2 tsp or 3g), black pepper (1/4 tsp or 0.5g), and red pepper flakes if using (1/2 tsp or 1g).

Step 4 | Combine and season
To the cooled bulgur, add diced tomatoes (1 cup or 180g), cucumber (3/4 cup or 100g), green onions (1/3 cup or 50g), chopped parsley (1 cup or 60g), and mint (1/4 cup or 15g). Pour the dressing over the salad and mix thoroughly to combine.

Step 5 | Let flavors meld
Allow the salad to sit for at least 10 minutes before serving, enabling the flavors to meld together.

NOTES

- For a gluten-free alternative, replace bulgur wheat with quinoa.
- The salad keeps well in the refrigerator for up to 2 days, making it ideal for meal prep.

SALADS & MEZZES

BAKED FETA WITH HONEY AND SESAME SEEDS, ALBANIA

This dish pairs the creamy texture of feta cheese with the floral sweetness of honey and the crunchy texture of sesame seeds, encapsulating the essence of Mediterranean culinary simplicity. Ideal as a unique appetizer or as a savory-sweet complement to any mezze platter.

METHOD OVEN
TIME 25 MINUTE
SERVING 4 PERSON
CALORIES 200

- ✓ Baking dish
- ✓ Oven
- ✓ Measuring spoons

INGREDIENTS

- 8 oz (226g) block of feta cheese
- 2 tablespoons (30ml) honey
- 1 tablespoon (9g) sesame seeds
- 1 tablespoon (15ml) olive oil
- Fresh thyme sprigs for garnish (optional)
- Crusty bread or pita for serving

INSTRUCTIONS

Step 1 | Preheat the oven
Set your oven to 400°F (200°C) to prepare for baking.

Step 2 | Prepare the cheese
Place the 8 oz (226g) block of feta cheese in a baking dish. Ensure the dish is snug enough to hold the cheese comfortably without too much space around it.

Step 3 | Add toppings:
Drizzle the feta evenly with 1 tablespoon (15ml) of olive oil. Then, generously pour 2 tablespoons (30ml) of honey over the feta, ensuring it is well coated. Sprinkle 1 tablespoon (9g) of sesame seeds over the honey-covered feta, pressing them lightly to adhere.

Step 4 | Bake the feta
Place the dish in the preheated oven and bake for about 15 minutes, or until the feta is slightly golden and begins to soften.

Step 5 | Garnish and serve
Remove the feta from the oven and allow it to cool slightly for 1-2 minutes. Garnish with fresh thyme sprigs if desired. Serve the baked feta warm with slices of crusty bread or pita for dipping.

NOTES

- **Adding a sprinkle of chili flakes** before baking can introduce a spicy element to the dish.

- **Opt for a higher-quality feta cheese** with good moisture content to prevent drying out during baking.

- **This dish is best enjoyed freshly baked** while the feta is still warm and creamy, to fully appreciate the melding of flavors.

SALADS & MEZZES

3 ROMAN ARTICHOKES (CARCIOFI ALLA ROMANA), ITALY

METHOD
SKILLET

TIME
1 HOUR

SERVING
4 PERSON

CALORIES
190

Carciofi alla Romana reflects Roman culinary tradition, offering tender artichokes braised with fresh herbs and citrus, perfect as a side that complements any meal with Italian flair.

- ✓ Knife
- ✓ Cutting board
- ✓ Large pan or pot with a lid
- ✓ Measuring cups and spoons
- ✓ Spoon
- ✓ Small bowl

INGREDIENTS

- 4 large globe artichokes
- 2 lemons, halved (to prevent browning of the artichokes)
- 60 ml (1/4 cup / 2 fl oz) **extra virgin olive oil**
- 1 teaspoon (5 ml / about 5g) **minced garlic**
- 30 ml (2 tbsp / 1 fl oz) **fresh lemon juice**
- 15g (1/4 cup / about 0.5 oz) **finely chopped fresh parsley**
- 10g (2 tbsp / about 0.35 oz) **finely chopped fresh mint**
- 5g (1 tsp / 0.18 oz) **sea salt**
- 2.5g (1/2 tsp / 0.09 oz) **freshly ground black pepper**
- 120 ml (1/2 cup / 4 fl oz) **dry white wine**
- 120 ml (1/2 cup / 4 fl oz) **water**

INSTRUCTIONS

Step 1 | Prepare the artichokes
Remove the tough outer leaves until you reach the softer, lighter green leaves. Trim the tops and stems to about 2.5 cm (1 inch). Rub all cut surfaces with a lemon half.

Step 2 | Remove the choke
Open the leaves slightly to expose the center. Remove the fuzzy choke with a spoon, careful not to break the leaves. Rub again with lemon.

Step 3 | Prepare the herb mixture
In a small bowl, mix 1 tsp minced garlic, 30 ml (2 tbsp) lemon juice, 15g (1/4 cup) parsley, 10g (2 tbsp) mint, 5g (1 tsp) salt, and 2.5g (1/2 tsp) black pepper.

Step 4 | Stuff the artichokes:
Insert the herb paste into the center and between the leaves of each artichoke.

Step 5 | Braise the artichokes:
Heat 60 ml (1/4 cup) olive oil in a large pan over medium heat. Place artichokes stem side up, cook for 5 minutes until the bottoms start to brown. Add 120 ml (1/2 cup) white wine and 120 ml (1/2 cup) water, cover, reduce heat to low, and braise for 35-40 minutes until tender. Add more water if needed.

Step 6 | Serve
Transfer to a serving platter, spoon over the cooking liquid.

NOTES

- Select artichokes that feel heavy for their size with tightly packed leaves for the best flavor and texture.

- The cooking liquid makes an excellent sauce for drizzling over the dish or as a dipping sauce for bread.

- Carciofi alla Romana can be enjoyed hot or at room temperature, adding versatility to its serving options.

- Serve hot or at room temperature for flexidle serving options

SALADS & MEZZES

4 ROASTED PEPPERS WITH GARLIC AND PARSLEY, ITALY

INGREDIENTS

- 4 large red bell peppers (about 2 pounds or 900 grams)
- 4 cloves garlic, finely chopped
- 1/4 cup (about 15 grams or 0.53 ounces) fresh parsley, finely chopped
- 2 tbsp (30 ml or 1 fl oz) extra virgin olive oil
- Salt, to taste
- Freshly ground black pepper, to taste

METHOD ROASTING
TIME 45 MINUTE
SERVING 4 PERSON
CALORIES 120

From the heart of the Piedmont region, these Roasted Peppers with Garlic and Parsley bring a mix of sweet and savory notes, enriched with aromatic garlic and parsley, making them perfect as an appetizer or vibrant side dish.

- ✓ Mixing bowl
- ✓ Baking sheet
- ✓ Parchment paper
- ✓ Serving dish
- ✓ Kitchen towel or paper bag

INSTRUCTIONS

Step 1 | Preheat and prepare
Set your oven to 400°F (200°C). Line a baking sheet with parchment paper.

Step 2 | Roast the peppers
Place washed and dried bell peppers on the sheet. Roast for 30 minutes, turning occasionally, until the skins are charred.

Step 3 | Steam and peel
Remove peppers from the oven, cover with a towel or place in a paper bag for about 10 minutes to loosen the skins. Then peel, remove stems and seeds, and slice into strips.

Step 4 | Mix and season
In a mixing bowl, combine the pepper strips with 4 chopped garlic cloves and 1/4 cup (about 15 grams) chopped parsley. Drizzle with 2 tbsp (30 ml) olive oil. Season with salt and black pepper to taste, and toss.

Step 5 | Serve
Place the pepper mixture in a serving dish. Let sit for 10 minutes to allow flavors to blend before serving.

NOTES

- Sprinkle chili flakes before serving for an extra kick.
- Gluten-free and vegan-friendly.
- Can be prepared ahead and stored in the refrigerator; bring to room temperature before serving.

SALADS & MEZZES

5 QUINOA TABBOULEH WITH FRESH HERBS AND LEMON, SYRIA

This Quinoa Tabbouleh offers a delightful and nutritious twist on the traditional Middle Eastern salad, using quinoa as a gluten-free alternative to bulgur wheat. It's infused with fresh parsley, mint, and a zesty lemon dressing, making it a refreshing side or a fulfilling light meal.

METHOD: MIXING
TIME: 30 MINUTE
SERVING: 4 PERSON
CALORIES: 280

- Fork
- Chef's knife
- Medium saucepan with lid
- Chopping board
- Large mixing bowl
- Whisk
- Small bowl

INGREDIENTS

- 1 cup (170g) quinoa, rinsed
- 2 cups (473ml) water
- 1 large bunch fresh parsley, finely chopped (about 2 cups or 60g)
- 1/2 cup (15g) fresh mint leaves, finely chopped
- 4 medium tomatoes, diced (about 2 cups or 300g)
- 1 medium cucumber, diced (about 1 cup or 150g)
- 3 green onions, thinly sliced (45g)
- 1/4 cup (60ml) olive oil
- 1/4 cup (60ml) fresh lemon juice
- Zest of 1 lemon
- Salt and pepper, to taste

NOTES
- Chill in the refrigerator for an hour before serving for the best flavor.
- Store in an airtight container in the refrigerator for up to 3 days.

INSTRUCTIONS

Step 1 | Cook the quinoa
Place the rinsed quinoa (170g) and water (2 cups or 473ml) in a medium saucepan over medium-high heat. Bring to a boil, then reduce heat to low, cover, and simmer for 15 minutes, or until the quinoa is tender and the water is absorbed. Fluff with a fork and let cool to room temperature.

Step 2 | Prepare the vegetables
While the quinoa cools, finely chop the parsley (about 2 cups or 60g) and mint leaves (1/2 cup or 15g). Dice the tomatoes (2 cups or 300g) and cucumber (1 cup or 150g), and thinly slice the green onions (45g).

Step 3 | Make the dressing
Whisk together the olive oil (1/4 cup or 60ml), fresh lemon juice (1/4 cup or 60ml), and lemon zest in a small bowl. Season with salt and pepper to taste.

Step 4 | Combine and dress
In a large mixing bowl, combine the cooled quinoa, chopped parsley, mint, diced tomatoes, cucumber, and sliced green onions. Drizzle the dressing over the mixture and toss to combine.

Step 5 | Let flavors meld
Let the tabbouleh sit for at least 10 minutes before serving to allow the flavors to meld.

- Consider adding dill or cilantro for a different flavor profile.

SALADS & MEZZES

6 GREEN OLIVE SALAD WITH LEMON AND PARSLEY, TURKEY

Experience the fresh, zesty flavors of the Mediterranean with this Turkish Green Olive Salad. This vibrant dish combines green olives with the tang of lemon and the freshness of parsley, creating a refreshing side perfect for any mezze platter or as a complement to a variety of main dishes. Its simplicity and robust flavors encapsulate the spirit of Turkish cuisine.

METHOD: MIXING
TIME: 15 MINUTE
SERVING: 4 PERSON
CALORIES: 150

- Chef's knife
- Citrus juicer (optional)
- Cutting board
- Mixing bow
- Measuring cups and spoons

INGREDIENTS

- 1 cup (150g) green olives, pitted and sliced
- 1 medium red onion, thinly sliced
- 1 large lemon, zest and juice
- 1/2 cup (30g) fresh parsley, finely chopped
- 2 tablespoons (30ml) extra virgin olive oil
- 1 clove garlic, minced
- 1/2 teaspoon (2g) ground cumin
- 1/4 teaspoon (1g) red pepper flakes
- Salt and black pepper, to taste

INSTRUCTIONS

Step 1 | Prepare ingredients
Pit and slice the green olives (150g). Thinly slice the red onion and mince the garlic clove.

Step 2 | Combine primary ingredients
In a large mixing bowl, add the sliced green olives and red onion.

Step 3 | Add zest and lemon juice
Zest the lemon into the bowl, then cut the lemon in half and squeeze its juice (measure to ensure approximately 2 tablespoons or 30ml) over the olives and onions, avoiding seeds.

Step 4 | Incorporate herbs and spices
Add the finely chopped parsley (1/2 cup or 30g), drizzle with extra virgin olive oil (2 tablespoons or 30ml), and sprinkle in the minced garlic, ground cumin (1/2 teaspoon or 2g), and red pepper flakes (1/4 teaspoon or 1g).

Step 5 | Season and mix
Season with salt and freshly ground black pepper, considering the natural saltiness of the olives. Gently toss all ingredients to ensure they are well coated with the dressing.

Step 6 | Let flavors meld
Allow the salad to sit for about 10 minutes before serving to let the flavors blend and intensify.

- **Variations:** Consider adding diced tomatoes or cucumber for extra texture and freshness.

- **Serving suggestion:** Serve as part of a mezze platter, along with other dishes like hummus, baba ganoush, and warm pita bread.

NOTES

- **Milder onion flavor:** If you prefer a less intense onion flavor, soak the sliced onions in ice water for 10 minutes before adding them to the salad.

- **Make-ahead:** This salad can be prepared ahead and stored in the refrigerator for up to 2 days, though it is best enjoyed fresh.

SALADS & MEZZES

7 BEET AND YOGURT SALAD (PANCAR SALATASI), TURKEY

METHOD
Mixing
Roasting

TIME
1 hour
15 minutes

SERVING
4 person

CALORIES
130

Experience the refreshing and earthy sweetness of this Turkish Beet and Yogurt Salad, a vibrant dish that blends roasted beets with tangy yogurt. Enhanced with Mediterranean herbs and a touch of spices, this mezze is perfect for adding a burst of color and flavor to any meal.

- ✓ Aluminum foil
- ✓ Mixing bowl
- ✓ Gloves (optional for handling beets)
- ✓ Baking shee
- ✓ Oven
- ✓ Measuring cups and spoons
- ✓ Knife
- ✓ Cutting board

INGREDIENTS

- 4 medium beets (about 1 lb or 450g), scrubbed
- 1 cup (245g) Greek yogurt
- 2 cloves garlic, minced
- 1 tablespoon (15ml) olive oil
- 2 tablespoons (30ml) lemon juice
- 1/2 teaspoon (1g) salt
- 1/4 teaspoon (0.5g) black pepper
- 1/4 teaspoon (0.5g) ground cumin
- 2 tablespoons (8g) fresh dill, finely chopped
- 1 tablespoon (4g) fresh mint, finely chopped
- 1 tablespoon (10g) walnuts, chopped (optional)

NOTES

- **Flavor adjustments:** Depending on the natural sweetness of the beets, adjust the lemon juice or add a pinch of sugar to balance the flavors to your taste.

- **Vegan option:** For a vegan version, substitute Greek yogurt with a suitable plant-based yogurt and adjust the seasoning as needed.

INSTRUCTIONS

Step 1 | Roast the beets
Preheat your oven to 400°F (200°C). Wrap each beet individually in aluminum foil and place them on a baking sheet. Roast for about 1 hour or until tender and easily pierced with a fork.

Step 2 | Prepare the beets
Allow the roasted beets to cool enough to handle. Then, peel them using gloves to avoid staining your hands, and dice into small cubes (1 lb or 450g).

Step 3 | Make the dressing
In a medium mixing bowl, combine Greek yogurt (1 cup or 245g), minced garlic, olive oil (1 tbsp or 15ml), lemon juice (2 tbsp or 30ml), salt (1/2 tsp or 1g), pepper (1/4 tsp or 0.5g), and ground cumin (1/4 tsp or 0.5g). Mix well to integrate the flavors.

Step 4 | Combine and chill
Add the diced beets to the yogurt mixture. Gently fold until the beets are fully coated with the dressing. Refrigerate the salad for at least 30 minutes to allow flavors to meld.

Step 5 | Garnish and serve
Before serving, garnish the salad with freshly chopped dill (2 tbsp or 8g), mint (1 tbsp or 4g), and optional walnuts (1 tbsp or 10g) for added texture and flavor.

- **Make-ahead:** This salad can be prepared in advance and is ideal for meal prep, as the flavors develop more intensely over time.

SALADS & MEZZES

8 TUNA AND POTATO SALAD, SPAIN

INGREDIENTS

- 1 pound (450g) potatoes, peeled and diced
- 1 can tuna in olive oil, drained and flaked (4 ounces or 113g)
- 1 medium carrot, peeled and diced (about 1/2 cup or 60g)
- 1/2 cup (70g) frozen peas, thawed
- 1/4 cup (60g) roasted red peppers, diced
- 3 tablespoons mayonnaise (more if desired)
- 1 tablespoon extra virgin olive oil
- 1 teaspoon white wine vinegar
- Salt and pepper, to taste
- 2 hard-boiled eggs, chopped
- 2 tablespoons capers, drained (optional)
- Fresh parsley, chopped for garnish

METHOD: MIXING BOILING
TIME: 35 MINUTE
SERVING: 4 PERSON
CALORIES: 290

Andalusian Tuna and Potato Salad, also known as Ensaladilla Rusa, is a popular dish across Spain, beloved for its comforting blend of creamy textures and hearty flavors. This salad combines tender potatoes, flaky tuna, and crisp vegetables, all enveloped in a creamy mayonnaise dressing, making it a perfect dish for gatherings or a satisfying appetizer.

- 1 small mixing bowl
- 1 large mixing bowl
- 2 pots (for boiling vegetables and eggs)
- Whisk
- 1 colander
- Measuring cups and spoons
- Knife and cutting board

INSTRUCTIONS

Step 1 | Prepare the vegetables
Boil the diced potatoes (1 pound or 450g) in salted water until fork-tender, about 10-12 minutes. Simultaneously, boil the diced carrot in a separate pot for about 5 minutes, adding the peas during the last minute. Drain both and let them cool.

Step 2 | Combine salad ingredients
n a large mixing bowl, mix the cooled potatoes, carrots, peas, flaked tuna (1 can or 113g), and diced roasted red peppers.

Step 3 | Prepare the dressing
In a small bowl, whisk together the mayonnaise, olive oil (1 tbsp), and white wine vinegar (1 tsp) until smooth. Season with salt and pepper to taste.

Step 4 | Dress the salad
Pour the dressing over the potato mixture, stirring gently to coat everything evenly. Add more mayonnaise if needed for desired consistency.

Step 5 | Add eggs and optional ingredients
Fold in the chopped hard-boiled eggs and capers (2 tbsp, optional), ensuring even distribution.

Step 5 | Chill and serve
Cover and refrigerate the salad for at least 1 hour to meld the flavors. Before serving, stir gently and garnish with fresh parsley. Adjust seasoning if necessary.

NOTES

- **Lighter version**: For a healthier alternative, substitute mayonnaise with Greek yogurt or a blend of mayo and yogurt.
- **Make-ahead**: To prepare ahead, store the cooked ingredients separately in the refrigerator and combine them with the dressing about an hour before serving.
- **Customization**: Enhance this salad with additional ingredients like olives, pickles, or fresh herbs such as dill or chives for varied flavors and textures.

SOUP

SOUP

EGGPLANT AND CHICKPEA STEW WITH CUMIN, SYRIA

Infused with cumin, coriander, and a touch of cayenne, this hearty stew pairs the creamy textures of eggplant with protein-rich chickpeas for a comforting meal that satisfies vegetarians and meat-eaters alike.

METHOD
POT

TIME
55 MINUTE

SERVING
4 PERSON

CALORIES
295

- Wooden spoon
- Chef's knife
- Large pot
- Cutting board
- Measuring cups and spoons

INGREDIENTS

- Eggplants, cut into cubes: 2 medium (about 1 lb or 450g)
- Chickpeas, drained and rinsed: 1 can (15 oz or 425g)
- Large onion, finely chopped: 1 (about 8 oz or 225g)
- Garlic cloves, minced: 3
- Large tomatoes, diced: 2 (about 1 lb or 450g)
- Ground cumin: 1 tsp (2g)
- Ground coriander: 1/2 tsp (1g)
- Cayenne pepper: 1/4 tsp (0.5g)
- Olive oil: 1/4 cup (2 fl oz or 60 ml)
- Vegetable broth: 2 cups (480 ml)
- Salt and pepper to taste
- Fresh cilantro or parsley for garnish
- Lemon, cut into wedges for serving: 1

INSTRUCTIONS

Step 1 | Sauté Eggplant
Heat half of the olive oil (1 fl oz or 30 ml) in a large pot over medium heat. Sauté the eggplant cubes until golden and softened, about 10 minutes. Remove and set aside.

Step 2 | Sauté Onions and Garlic
In the same pot, add the remaining olive oil (1 fl oz or 30 ml). Sauté the chopped onions (1 large) until translucent, about 3 minutes. Add the minced garlic (3 cloves) and cook for another minute until fragrant.

Step 3 | Add Spices and Tomatoes
Stir in the ground cumin (1 tsp / 2g), ground coriander (1/2 tsp / 1g), and cayenne pepper (1/4 tsp / 0.5g), cooking for a minute to release the flavors. Add the diced tomatoes (2 large / about 1 lb or 450g) and cook until saucy, about 5 minutes.

Step 4 | Combine Ingredients
Return the sautéed eggplant to the pot, add the drained chickpeas (1 can / 15 oz or 425g), and pour in the vegetable broth (2 cups / 480 ml). Bring to a simmer, cover, and cook for 25 minutes, stirring occasionally.

Step 5 | Season and Serve
Season the stew with salt and pepper to taste. Serve hot, garnished with fresh cilantro or parsley, and lemon wedges on the side.

NOTES

- **Roasting Tip:** Roast the eggplant at 400°F (200°C) for 20 minutes before adding to the stew for a deeper flavor.
- **Adjust Consistency:** Adjust the consistency with more vegetable broth if desired.

SOUP

MINESTRA SOUP WITH BEANS AND GREENS, CORSICA

METHOD — POT
TIME — 1 HOUR 30 MINUTES
SERVING — 6 PERSON
CALORIES — 210

Embark on a culinary journey to Corsica with this rustic Minestra Soup, a warming blend of beans and greens that captures the essence of the island's hearty flavors and culinary traditions. It's a nourishing meal that brings comfort and tradition to your table.

- ✓ Large soup pot
- ✓ Chopping board
- ✓ Chef's knife
- ✓ Wooden spoon
- ✓ Can opener
- ✓ Cheese grater (optional)

INGREDIENTS

- 2 tbsp olive oil (1 fl oz or 30 ml)
- 1 large onion, diced (about 7 oz or 200 g)
- 3 cloves garlic, minced (about 0.5 oz or 15 g)
- 2 carrots, peeled and diced (about 5.3 oz or 150 g)
- 2 stalks celery, diced (about 3.9 oz or 110 g)
- 8 cups vegetable stock
- 1 can cannellini beans, drained and rinsed (15 oz or 425 g)
- 1 can kidney beans, drained and rinsed (15 oz or 425 g)
- 1 tsp dried thyme
- 1 bay leaf
- 1 bunch Swiss chard, stems removed and leaves chopped (about 10.6 oz or 300 g)
- 1 bunch spinach, stems removed and leaves chopped (about 8.8 oz or 250 g)
- Salt and pepper to taste
- Freshly grated Pecorino cheese for serving (optional)

INSTRUCTIONS

Step 1 | Sauté Onions and Garli
Heat the olive oil (1 fl oz or 30 ml) in a large soup pot over medium heat. Add the diced onion (7 oz or 200 g) and sauté until translucent, about 5 minutes. Add the minced garlic (0.5 oz or 15 g) and cook for another minute until fragrant.

Step 2 | Add Vegetables
Add the diced carrots (5.3 oz or 150 g) and diced celery (3.9 oz or 110 g) to the pot. Cook for another 5 minutes until the vegetables start to soften.

Step 3 | Add Stock and Beans
Pour in the vegetable stock (8 cups) and bring to a boil. Add the cannellini beans (15 oz or 425 g), kidney beans (15 oz or 425 g), dried thyme (1 tsp), and bay leaf. Reduce to a simmer, cover, and cook for 40 minutes.

Step 4 | Add Greens
Stir in the chopped Swiss chard (10.6 oz or 300 g) and spinach (8.8 oz or 250 g). Season with salt and pepper to taste. Continue to simmer for 15-20 minutes until the greens are tender.

Step 5 | Serve
Remove and discard the bay leaf. Serve the soup hot, optionally topped with freshly grated Pecorino cheese.

NOTES

- Homemade vegetable stock enhances the flavor.
- Store soup in the refrigerator for up to 3 days or freeze for up to 3 months.
- For a vegan version, omit Pecorino or substitute with a vegan cheese.

SOUP

CALDO VERDE WITH CHORIZO AND KALE, PORTUGAL

INGREDIENTS

- 1/2 pound chorizo sausage, sliced (8 oz or 225g)
- 1 large onion, chopped (about 1 cup or 200g)
- 2 cloves garlic, minced
- 6 medium potatoes, peeled and diced (2 lbs or 900g)
- 4 cups chicken or vegetable broth (1 liter)
- 4 cups water (1 liter)
- 1 teaspoon salt (5g)
- 1/2 teaspoon black pepper (2g)
- 1 bunch kale, stems removed and leaves thinly sliced (about 1/2 pound or 225g)
- 2 tablespoons olive oil (30ml)

METHOD POT
TIME 45 MINUTES
SERVING 4 PERSON
CALORIES 470

Caldo Verde, a quintessential Portuguese soup, melds the smoky flavors of chorizo with the earthiness of kale and the heartiness of potatoes. This savory dish is a staple in Portuguese cuisine, offering warmth and comfort in every spoonful.

- ✓ Large pot
- ✓ Cutting board
- ✓ Chef's knife
- ✓ Immersion blender or potato masher

INSTRUCTIONS

Step 1 |
Heat olive oil (30ml) in a large pot over medium heat. Sauté chorizo until it starts to brown, about 5 minutes.

Step 2 |
Add onion and garlic; cook until onion is translucent and fragrant, about 3-4 minutes.

Step 3 |
Add potatoes and pour in broth and water. Season with salt (5g) and pepper (2g). Bring to a boil, then reduce to a simmer until potatoes are tender, about 20 minutes.

Step 4 |
Partially puree the soup in the pot using an immersion blender, or mash the potatoes with a potato masher for texture.

Step 5 |
Stir in kale and simmer for another 5 minutes until wilted and tender. Adjust seasoning if necessary.

Step 6 |
Serve hot, optionally with a slice of crusty bread.

NOTES

- For extra heat, use hot chorizo or add red pepper flakes.
- For a vegetarian version, omit chorizo and opt for vegetable broth

SOUP

4 ROASTED CARROT SOUP WITH GINGER AND ORANGE, SPAIN

Enjoy the delightful blend of flavors of the Roasted Carrot Soup, featuring the sweetness of roasted carrots, the zest of orange, and the warmth of ginger. Perfect for a comforting dinner or an elegant appetizer.

METHOD POT | **TIME** 1 HOUR | **SERVING** 4 PERSON | **CALORIES** 190

- ✓ Baking sheet
- ✓ Large pot
- ✓ Knife and cutting board
- ✓ Measuring cups and spoons
- ✓ Immersion blender or standard blender

INGREDIENTS

- Carrots, peeled and chopped: 2 pounds (907g)
- Olive oil: 2 tablespoons (30ml)
- Salt and pepper to taste
- Vegetable broth: 4 cups (960ml)
- Freshly squeezed orange juice: 1 cup (240ml)
- Fresh ginger, grated: 2 tablespoons (15g)
- Medium onion, diced: 1
- Garlic cloves, minced: 3
- Ground cumin: 1 teaspoon (2g)
- Ground coriander: 1/2 teaspoon (1g)
- Heavy cream (optional, for garnish): 1/4 cup (60ml)
- Fresh herbs such as parsley or cilantro, for garnish

INSTRUCTIONS

Step 1 | Roast Carrots
Preheat the oven to 425°F (220°C). Toss the chopped carrots (2 pounds / 907g) with 1 tablespoon of olive oil (15ml), salt, and pepper on a baking sheet. Roast for 25-30 minutes until tender and caramelized, stirring halfway through.

Step 2 | Sauté Onions
In a large pot, heat the remaining 1 tablespoon of olive oil (15ml) over medium heat. Sauté the diced onion (1 medium) until translucent, about 5 minutes.

Step 3 | Add Aromatics
Add the minced garlic (3 cloves), grated ginger (2 tablespoons / 15g), ground cumin (1 teaspoon / 2g), and ground coriander (1/2 teaspoon / 1g) to the pot. Cook for another minute until fragrant.

Step 4 | Combine Ingredients
Add the roasted carrots, vegetable broth (4 cups / 960ml), and freshly squeezed orange juice (1 cup / 240ml) to the pot. Simmer for 10 minutes.

Step 5 | Blend Soup
Blend the soup using an immersion blender or in batches with a standard blender until smooth. Adjust the thickness with more broth or water if needed. Season with salt and pepper to taste.

Step 6 | Serve
Serve the soup hot, garnished with a drizzle of heavy cream (1/4 cup / 60ml) and fresh herbs if desired.

NOTES

- For a vegan version, omit the heavy cream or substitute with a plant-based alternative
- The combination of carrots, orange, and ginger offers a harmonious blend of sweet, acidic, and spicy flavors.

SOUP

5 | LENTIL AND PUMPKIN STEW, SICILY

METHOD — POT
TIME — 1 HOUR
SERVING — 4 PERSON
CALORIES — 330

Embrace the comforting flavors of Sicily with this Lentil and Pumpkin Stew. The earthy lentils and sweet pumpkin meld beautifully in a savory tomato base, enhanced with aromatic herbs and spices. This nutritious stew is perfect for a cozy, heart-warming dinner.

- Large pot
- Measuring cups and spoons
- Knife
- Cutting board

INGREDIENTS

- Green lentils, rinsed: 1 cup (190g / 6.7oz)
- Pumpkin, peeled and diced into 1/2-inch cubes: 2 cups (450g / 16oz)
- Large onion, finely chopped: 1
- Garlic cloves, minced: 3
- Olive oil: 2 tbsp (30ml)
- Diced tomatoes: 1 can (14 oz / 400g)
- Vegetable broth: 4 cups (960ml)
- Dried oregano: 1 tsp (1g)
- Crushed red pepper flakes: 1/2 tsp (1g)
- Salt and pepper to taste
- Fresh parsley, chopped for garnish: 2 tbsp (8g)

INSTRUCTIONS

Step 1 | Sauté Onions and Garlic
Heat olive oil (2 tbsp / 30ml) in a large pot over medium heat. Sauté the chopped onion (1 large) and minced garlic (3 cloves) until the onion is translucent, about 3-4 minutes.

Step 2 | Add Pumpkin
Add the diced pumpkin (2 cups / 450g / 16oz) and cook for 5 more minutes, stirring occasionally.

Step 3 | Mix in Lentils
Mix in the green lentils (1 cup / 190g / 6.7oz), ensuring they blend well with the vegetables.

Step 4 | Add Tomatoes and Broth
Pour in the diced tomatoes (1 can / 14 oz / 400g) and vegetable broth (4 cups / 960ml). Season with dried oregano (1 tsp / 1g), crushed red pepper flakes (1/2 tsp / 1g), salt, and pepper. Stir well.

Step 5 | Simmer Stew
Bring the mixture to a boil, then lower to a simmer. Cover and cook for 35 minutes or until the lentils and pumpkin are tender.

Step 6 | Adjust Consistency
Adjust the stew's consistency with more broth or water if needed. Season to taste.

Step 7 | Serve
Serve the stew hot, garnished with fresh parsley (2 tbsp / 8g).

NOTES

- Add chorizo or pancetta for a meaty version during the onion sauté.
- For a creamier texture, partially blend the stew before serving.
- Store in the refrigerator for up to 3 days or freeze for up to a month.
- Enhance flavor by roasting the pumpkin beforehand.

SOUP

6 ANDALUSIAN CHILLED ALMOND SOUP (AJO BLANCO), SPAIN

INGREDIENTS

- Blanched almonds: 1 cup (143g / 5oz)
- Cold water: 3 cups (710ml)
- Garlic clove, roughly chopped: 1
- White bread, crusts removed: 4 slices (120g / 4.2oz)
- Extra virgin olive oil: 3 tablespoons (45ml)
- Sherry vinegar: 2 tablespoons (30ml)
- Sea salt: 1 teaspoon (5g)
- Green grapes, halved: 1/2 cup (75g / 2.6oz)
- Fresh mint leaves for garnish (optional)

METHOD FRIDGE
TIME 2 HOURS 15 MINUTES
SERVING 4 PERSON
CALORIES 300

Delight in the refreshing taste of Andalusia with Ajo Blanco, a traditional chilled almond soup. This creamy blend of almonds, garlic, and bread, garnished with juicy green grapes, offers a delicious escape from the summer heat, embodying the essence of Mediterranean cuisine.

- ✓ Food processor or blender
- ✓ Measuring cups and spoons
- ✓ Fine sieve (optional)

INSTRUCTIONS

Step 1 | Soak Bread
Soak the bread slices in 1 cup (240ml) of water until soft.

Step 2 | Process Almonds and Garlic
In a blender or food processor, process the blanched almonds (143g / 5oz) and garlic (1 clove) to form a fine paste.

Step 3 | Add Bread
Squeeze excess water from the bread and add to the almond-garlic paste. Blend until smooth.

Step 4 | Blend with Oil and Vinegar
With the machine running, gradually add olive oil (45ml), then sherry vinegar (30ml), blending until creamy.

Step 5 | Incorporate Water and Seaso Slowly incorporate the remaining 2 cups (480ml) of cold water, blending until smooth. Stir in the sea salt (5g).

Step 6 | Strain Soup
For a smoother texture, strain the soup through a fine sieve, pressing the solids.

Step 7 | Chill Soup
Chill the soup in the refrigerator for at least 2 hours, or overnight for enhanced flavors.

Step 8 | Serve
Serve chilled, topped with halved green grapes (75g / 2.6oz) and a drizzle of olive oil. Garnish with fresh mint if using.

NOTES

- Use vegan bread for a vegan version of this soup.
- Toasting the almonds before blending can enhance the nutty flavor.
- Adjust the soup's thickness by adding more water if necessary.

SOUP

7 CHILLED AVOCADO AND CUCUMBER SOUP WITH MINT AND YOGURT, SPAIN

Cool off on warm days with this Chilled Avocado and Cucumber Soup, featuring the creamy texture of avocados, the freshness of cucumber, and the tang of Greek yogurt, all enhanced with mint. It's a refreshingly light appetizer that's as nourishing as it is delightful.

METHOD FRIDGE | **TIME** 15 MINUTE | **SERVING** 4 PERSON | **CALORIES** 200

- Blender
- Knife
- Bowls for serving
- Chopping board
- Measuring cups and spoon

INGREDIENTS

- Ripe avocados, peeled and pitted: 2 (approximately 450g / 16oz)
- Large cucumber, peeled and roughly chopped: 1 (approximately 450g / 16oz)
- Plain Greek yogurt: 1 1/2 cups (360ml)
- Fresh mint leaves, finely chopped, plus extra for garnish: 1/4 cup (15g)
- Freshly squeezed lemon juice: 2 tablespoons (30ml)
- Garlic clove, minced: 1
- Cold water: 2 cups (480ml)
- Salt and pepper: to taste
- Extra virgin olive oil for drizzling: optional

INSTRUCTIONS

Step 1 | Prepare the Avocados and Cucumber
Remove pits from avocados, scoop out the flesh, and roughly chop the peeled cucumber.

Step 2 | Blend Ingredients
In a blender, combine avocado (450g / 16oz), cucumber (450g / 16oz), Greek yogurt (360ml), mint (15g), lemon juice (30ml), and garlic. Blend until smooth.

Step 3 | Add Water
Gradually add cold water (480ml) while blending to achieve a creamy, pourable consistency.

Step 4 | Season
Season with salt and pepper to taste. Adjust flavor with more lemon juice if needed.

Step 5 | Chill Soup
Chill the soup in the refrigerator for at least 1 hour to enhance flavors.

Step 6 | Serve
Serve chilled in bowls, garnished with mint leaves and drizzled with olive oil if desired.

NOTES

- For a vegan option, replace Greek yogurt with a plant-based yogurt.
- Adjust soup thickness by altering the amount of water.
- The soup can be stored in the refrigerator for up to 2 days.
- Add a small jalapeño pepper to the blend for a spicy kick.

SOUP

8 GRILLED VEGETABLE GAZPACHO WITH FRESH BASIL, SPAIN

METHOD GRILL | **TIME** 30 MINUTE | **SERVING** 4 PERSON | **CALORIES** 120

Experience a refreshing twist on a classic Spanish soup with our Grilled Vegetable Gazpacho with Fresh Basil, where the smokiness of grilled vegetables meets the zesty flavors of fresh basil and ripe tomatoes, creating a perfect harmony of taste that's both invigorating and satisfying.

- Grill
- Large bowl
- Cutting board
- Blender or food processor
- Knife
- Measuring cups and spoons

INGREDIENTS

- Ripe tomatoes, quartered: 1 lb (450 g)
- Red bell pepper, halved and seeded: 1 medium
- Yellow bell pepper, halved and seeded: 1 medium
- Red onion, peeled and cut into wedges: 1 small
- Zucchini, sliced lengthwise: 1 medium
- Garlic, unpeeled: 2 cloves
- Extra virgin olive oil: 3 tbsp (45 ml)
- Cucumber, peeled and diced: 1
- Red wine vinegar: ¼ cup (60 ml)
- Fresh basil leaves, plus more for garnish: ¼ cup (15 g)
- Salt and freshly ground black pepper: to taste
- Smoked paprika: 1 tsp (2.5 g)
- Cumin: ½ tsp (1 g)
- Cold water: 2 cups (480 ml)
- Ice cubes: for serving

NOTES

- To enhance the flavors, consider adding a splash of sherry vinegar or topping with diced avocado and crumbled feta cheese.
- For a protein boost, add in some cooked and chilled shrimp or white beans.
- Gazpacho can be stored in an airtight container in the refrigerator for up to 3 days.

INSTRUCTIONS

Step 1 | Preheat Grill
Preheat your grill to medium-high heat.

Step 2 | Prep Vegetables
In a large bowl, toss the tomatoes (1 lb or 450 g), red bell pepper (1 medium), yellow bell pepper (1 medium), red onion (1 small), zucchini (1 medium), and garlic (2 cloves) with 2 tablespoons (30 ml) of olive oil, salt, and pepper.

Step 3 | Grill Vegetables
Place the vegetables on the grill and cook for about 5 minutes on each side, until they are nicely charred and softened. Grill the garlic for about 10 minutes, turning occasionally, until softened.

Step 4 | Cool and Prep Garlic
Once grilled, set aside the vegetables to cool slightly. Squeeze the garlic out of its skin and discard the skin.

Step 5 | Blend Gazpacho
In a blender or food processor, combine the grilled vegetables, grilled garlic, cucumber (1), red wine vinegar (¼ cup or 60 ml), fresh basil leaves (¼ cup or 15 g), remaining olive oil (1 tbsp or 15 ml), smoked paprika (1 tsp or 2.5 g), cumin (½ tsp or 1 g), and cold water (2 cups or 480 ml). Blend until smooth.

Step 6 | Adjust Seasoning
Taste and adjust the seasoning with additional salt, pepper, or vinegar as needed.

Step 7 | Chill Gazpacho
Chill the gazpacho in the refrigerator for at least 2 hours before serving.

Step 8 | Serve
Serve the chilled gazpacho in bowls with ice cubes, garnished with fresh basil leaves.

SPICES & SAUCES

SPICES & SAUCES

1 CHERMOULA SAUCE, NORTH AFRICA

INGREDIENTS

- 1 cup fresh parsley, ends trimmed (1.7 oz or 48g)
- 1 cup fresh cilantro, ends trimmed (1.7 oz or 48g)
- 1 to 2 cloves garlic
- 1 teaspoon coriander (ground) (0.1 oz or 2g)
- 1 teaspoon red pepper flakes (0.1 oz or 2g)
- ½ teaspoon paprika (0.05 oz or 1.5g)
- ½ teaspoon ground ginger (0.05 oz or 1.5g)
- ¼ teaspoon saffron threads, optional
- Kosher salt (to taste)
- 1 lemon, juice and zest (approximately 2 tbsp juice and 1 tsp zest)
- ¾ cup extra virgin olive oil (6 fl oz or 177 ml)

METHOD: FOOD PROCESSOR
TIME: 5 MINUTES
SERVING: 16 TABLESPOONS
CALORIES: 90

Chermoula brings a burst of vibrant Moroccan flavors to any dish. This zesty, herby sauce combines fresh parsley, cilantro, and spices with lemon and olive oil. It's versatile enough to enhance fish, meats, soups, and sandwiches, offering countless ways to elevate your meals.

✓ Food processor

INSTRUCTIONS

Step 1 |
In your food processor, combine parsley (1.7 oz or 48g), cilantro (1.7 oz or 48g), garlic, coriander (0.1 oz or 2g), red pepper flakes (0.1 oz or 2g), paprika (0.05 oz or 1.5g), ginger (0.05 oz or 1.5g), saffron threads, and a big pinch of salt.

Step 2 |
Add lemon juice (2 tbsp) and zest (1 tsp) to the mixture.

Step 3 |
Process the mixture while slowly drizzling in the olive oil (6 fl oz or 177 ml) through the feed tube. Pulse until well combined but still slightly textured.

Step 4 |
Taste and adjust the seasoning as needed.

NOTES

This recipe yields just over 1 cup of chermoula. Store it in an airtight container in the refrigerator and use within a week for best freshness and flavor. Enjoy it as a dynamic addition to a variety of dishes.

SPICES & SAUCES

OLIVE AND CAPERS TAPENADE, MALLORCA

This Mallorcan Olive and Capers Tapenade brings a burst of Mediterranean zest to your table. Combining the robust flavors of green olives with the briny sharpness of capers and aromatic herbs, this tapenade serves as an exquisite appetizer or a versatile enhancer to elevate any dish. Its ease of preparation makes it a perfect choice for quick, flavor-packed snacking or entertaining.

METHOD MIXING | **TIME** 10 MINUTES | **SERVING** 4 PERSON | **CALORIES** 175

- Food processor
- Cutting board spoons
- Measuring spoons
- Knife

INGREDIENTS

- 1 cup green olives, pitted (about 6 oz or 170g)
- 2 tbsp capers, drained (about 1 oz or 30ml)
- 2 cloves garlic, minced (about 1 tbsp or 15ml)
- 1/4 cup extra virgin olive oil (60ml)
- 1 tsp fresh lemon juice (5ml)
- 1/4 cup fresh parsley, chopped (about 1 oz or 28g)
- 1 tsp fresh thyme leaves (about 0.5g)
- 1/4 tsp red pepper flakes (optional) (about 1.25ml)
- Freshly ground black pepper, to taste

INSTRUCTIONS

Step 1 | Prepare the ingredients
Start by ensuring that the olives (1 cup or 170g) and capers (2 tbsp or 30ml) are well-drained to prevent excess moisture in the tapenade.

Step 2 | Blend the base
In a food processor, add the green olives, capers, and minced garlic (1 tbsp or 15ml). Pulse a few times until the ingredients are coarsely chopped.

Step 3 | Emulsify with oil
Continue to pulse while slowly drizzling in the extra virgin olive oil (1/4 cup or 60ml) until the mixture forms a coarse paste.

Step 4 | Incorporate herbs and seasonings
Add the fresh lemon juice (1 tsp or 5ml), chopped parsley (1/4 cup or 28g), thyme leaves (1 tsp or 0.5g), and red pepper flakes if using. Pulse to mix the herbs evenly throughout the tapenade. Season with freshly ground black pepper to taste.

Step 5 | Serve or store
Transfer the tapenade to a serving bowl. If not serving immediately, cover and refrigerate to let the flavors meld. Serve with crusty bread, crackers, or as a condiment for grilled meats or vegetables.

NOTES

- For a smoother texture, continue processing the tapenade until it reaches your desired consistency.

- Store the tapenade in an airtight container in the refrigerator for up to one week.

- This tapenade is naturally vegan, but always check the packaging of your olives and capers to ensure they are free of any animal products.

- Try a mix of green and black olives for a deeper, more nuanced flavor profile.

SPICES & SAUCES

3 TZATZIKI WITH CUCUMBER AND DILL, GREECE

METHOD — MIXING
TIME — 15 MINUTES
SERVING — 4 PERSON
CALORIES — 70

Immerse yourself in the refreshing and zesty flavors of Greece with this authentic Tzatziki recipe. This traditional Greek dip or sauce combines the coolness of cucumber, the aromatic allure of dill, and the rich tanginess of Greek yogurt, making it an essential component of any mezze platter or as a companion to grilled dishes.

- Grater
- Mixing bowl
- Garlic press (optional)
- Sieve
- Measuring spoons

INGREDIENTS

- 2 cups Greek yogurt (500g)
- 1 medium cucumber, grated (about 1 cup or 225g after draining)
- 2 cloves garlic, minced
- 2 tablespoons fresh dill, finely chopped (30ml)
- 1 tablespoon extra-virgin olive oil (15ml)
- 1 tablespoon lemon juice (15ml)
- 1/2 teaspoon salt (2.5ml)
- 1/4 teaspoon ground black pepper (1.25ml)

INSTRUCTIONS

Step 1 | Prepare the cucumber
Grate the cucumber and place it in a sieve set over a bowl. Sprinkle with salt and allow it to sit for 10 minutes to draw out moisture. Squeeze the grated cucumber to remove as much water as possible, ensuring a thicker, creamier tzatziki.

Step 2 | Mix the ingredients
In a mixing bowl, combine the strained Greek yogurt, minced garlic, chopped dill, olive oil, and lemon juice. Stir thoroughly to blend the ingredients well.

Step 3 | Combine cucumber with yogurt mixture
Add the drained grated cucumber to the yogurt mixture. Season with salt and black pepper. Mix well to ensure even distribution of ingredients.

Step 4 | Chill to meld flavors
Cover the bowl with plastic wrap and refrigerate for at least 1 hour. This resting period allows the flavors to meld together, enhancing the overall taste of the tzatziki.

Step 5 | Final touches before serving
Give the tzatziki a final stir before serving. Adjust the seasoning if necessary, and drizzle with a little more olive oil if desired.

NOTES

- For optimal flavor and texture, use full-fat Greek yogurt. For an even thicker tzatziki, consider straining the yogurt overnight through cheesecloth.
- Serve the tzatziki chilled with pita bread, fresh vegetables, or as a cooling sauce alongside grilled meats.
- This dish can be prepared a day ahead, making it perfect for gatherings where time management is key.

SPICES & SAUCES

4 POMEGRANATE GLAZE

INGREDIENTS

- 1/2 cup pomegranate juice (about 4 oz or 120ml)
- 2 tbsp honey (30ml)
- 1 tbsp balsamic vinegar (15ml)

METHOD POT
TIME 15 MINUTES
SERVING MAKES ABOUT 1/2 CUP
CALORIES 50

This rich and tangy Pomegranate Glaze is a versatile addition to your culinary repertoire, ideal for drizzling over grilled meats, roasted vegetables, or enhancing the flavor profile of salads. Its combination of pomegranate's natural tartness with the sweetness of honey and the depth of balsamic vinegar creates a delightful condiment that elevates any dish.

- ✓ Small saucepan
- ✓ Whisk
- ✓ Measuring cups and spoons

INSTRUCTIONS

Step 1 | Combine ingredients
In a small saucepan, combine pomegranate juice (1/2 cup or 120ml), honey (2 tbsp or 30ml), and balsamic vinegar (1 tbsp or 15ml).

Step 2 | Simmer
Place the saucepan over medium heat and bring the mixture to a simmer. Stir frequently to ensure the honey dissolves completely.

Step 3 | Reduce
Allow the mixture to simmer gently, stirring occasionally, until it reduces by about half and thickens to a syrup-like consistency, approximately 10-15 minutes.

Step 4 | Cool and store
Remove the glaze from heat and let it cool to room temperature. It will thicken further as it cools. Store in an airtight container in the refrigerator for up to 2 weeks.

NOTES

- **Serving suggestions:** Try this glaze with lamb, duck, or grilled salmon for a delightful flavor boost. It can also be used as a dressing base for salads or a decadent drizzle over soft cheeses.

- **Variations:** For a spicier kick, add a pinch of crushed red pepper flakes during the simmering process.

SPICES & SAUCES

5 ANATOLIAN ROASTED RED PEPPER HUMMUS WITH PITA CHIPS, TURKEY

Dive into the rich and smoky flavors of Anatolia with this Roasted Red Pepper Hummus, paired delightfully with crispy homemade pita chips. This dish combines the earthy tones of roasted bell peppers with the smooth texture of chickpeas, elevated by a touch of tahini and a zest of lemon, creating a perfect starter for any Mediterranean-inspired meal.

METHOD MIXING | **TIME** 25 MINUTE | **SERVING** 6 PERSON | **CALORIES** 290

✓ Baking sheet
✓ Food processor
✓ Garlic press (optional)
✓ Measuring cups and spoon

INGREDIENTS

- Chickpeas, canned, drained and rinsed (15 oz or 425g)
- Red bell peppers, roasted and peeled (2 large)
- Tahini (1/4 cup or 60ml)
- Garlic cloves, minced (2)
- Fresh lemon juice (3 tbsp or 45ml)
- Extra virgin olive oil (2 tbsp or 30ml), plus extra for drizzling
- Ground cumin (1 tsp or 2g)
- Paprika (1/2 tsp or 1g)
- Sea salt, to taste
- Ground black pepper, to taste
- Whole wheat pita bread, cut into rounds (4)
- Olive oil spray, for pita chips
- Sea salt, for pita chips

INSTRUCTIONS

Step 1 | Prepare pita chips
Preheat your oven to 400°F (200°C). Cut the pita bread into triangles and arrange them on a baking sheet. Lightly spray with olive oil and sprinkle with sea salt. Bake for 8-10 minutes or until crispy and golden (4 rounds). Remove and let cool.

Step 2 | Blend hummus ingredients
In a food processor, combine roasted red peppers, chickpeas (15 oz), tahini (1/4 cup), minced garlic (2 cloves), lemon juice (3 tbsp), olive oil (2 tbsp), cumin (1 tsp), paprika (1/2 tsp), sea salt, and black pepper. Blend until smooth, adjusting the thickness by adding water if needed (1 tbsp at a time).

Step 3 | Adjust seasoning and serve
Taste the hummus and adjust the seasoning with additional salt, lemon juice, or spices as preferred. Transfer the hummus to a serving bowl, drizzle with extra olive oil, and sprinkle with paprika for garnish. Serve with the pita chips.

NOTES

- **Enhance flavor:** For an even smokier taste, char the bell peppers over an open flame before peeling.
- **Storage tips:** Store the hummus in an airtight container in the refrigerator for up to 5 days.
- **Consistency adjustments:** Customize the thickness by varying the amount of water added during blending.
- **Chickpea options:** Substitute canned chickpeas with about 1 3/4 cups of cooked chickpeas if preferred.

TAHINI DRESSING, CYPRUS

METHOD: MIXING
TIME: 10 MINUTE
SERVING: 4 PERSON
CALORIES: 100

Tahini, a paste made from ground sesame seeds, is a staple in Middle Eastern cooking. Its use dates back to ancient times, making it one of the region's oldest condiments. This simple Tahini Dressing blends the nutty flavor of tahini with the zest of lemon and the pungency of garlic, creating a versatile and flavorful dressing perfect for enhancing the taste of salads, grilled vegetables, or as a drizzle over meats.

- Small bowl
- Whisk
- Measuring cups and spoons

INGREDIENTS

- 1/3 cup Tahini (approximately 80 ml)
- 1 Garlic clove, minced
- 2 tablespoons Lemon juice (about 30 ml)
- 3 tablespoons Water (about 45 ml)
- 1 tablespoon Olive oil (about 15 ml)
- Salt, to taste

INSTRUCTIONS

Step 1 | Prepare the base
In a small bowl, whisk together the tahini (1/3 cup or 80 ml) and minced garlic (1 clove).

Step 2 | Add liquids
Incorporate the lemon juice (2 tablespoons or 30 ml), water (3 tablespoons or 45 ml), and olive oil (1 tablespoon or 15 ml) until the mixture is smooth.

Step 3 | Season
Add salt to taste. Adjust the consistency by adding more water if needed to achieve a creamy but pourable texture.

NOTES

- For a thinner consistency, gradually add more water while whisking until the desired texture is achieved.
- This dressing can be stored in the refrigerator for up to one week in an airtight container.
- Try adding a pinch of cumin or paprika for a slightly spicy and aromatic twist.

SPICES & SAUCES

7 — PESTO GENOVESE WITH WALNUT AND MINT, ITALY

INGREDIENTS

- Fresh basil leaves: 2 cups (48g)
- Fresh mint leaves: 1/2 cup (12g)
- Walnuts: 1/3 cup (40g), toasted
- Grated Parmigiano-Reggiano cheese: 1/2 cup (45g)
- Garlic: 2 cloves (6g)
- Extra virgin olive oil: 2/3 cup (160ml)
- Fresh lemon juice: 1 tbsp (15ml)
- Salt: 1/2 tsp (3g)
- Black pepper: 1/4 tsp (0.5g)

METHOD: MIXING
TIME: 10 MINUTE
SERVING: 4 PERSON
CALORIES: 390

This innovative twist on the traditional Pesto Genovese blends the classic flavors of fresh basil with the refreshing zest of mint and the deep, earthy undertones of walnuts. This recipe provides a deliciously green, nutty sauce that enhances any dish, making it a perfect companion for pasta, sandwiches, or as a vibrant garnish for soups and salads.

- ✓ Food processor
- ✓ Skillet
- ✓ Measuring cups and spoons
- ✓ Kitchen towel or paper towels
- ✓ Airtight container (for storage)

INSTRUCTIONS

Step 1 | Toast Walnuts
Toast walnuts in a dry skillet over medium heat until fragrant (3-4 mins). Let cool.

Step 2 | Prepare Leaves
Wash and thoroughly dry basil and mint leaves.

Step 3 | Process Garlic and Nuts
Pulse garlic and walnuts in the food processor until finely chopped.

Step 4 | Add Leaves
Incorporate basil and mint, pulsing to coarsely chop

Step 5 | Blend with Oil
Stream olive oil into the processor while it runs, blending until smooth.

Step 6 | Mix Final Ingredients
Add cheese, lemon juice, salt, and pepper; pulse to combine.

Step 7 | Adjust Seasoning
Taste and adjust flavors as desired.

Step 8 | Store
If storing, place in an airtight container, cover surface with plastic wrap, and refrigerate.

NOTES

- **Color Preservation:** Blanch basil before processing to keep pesto green.

- **Nut-Free Option:** Substitute walnuts with pine nuts or omit nuts.

- **Vegan Adaptation:** Use nutritional yeast instead of Parmesan cheese to replicate the cheesy flavor.

SPICES & SAUCES

8 | LEMON FETA VINAIGRETTE

This Lemon Feta Vinaigrette is a creamy and tangy dressing that perfectly complements salads with its rich flavor. Blending the feta into the vinaigrette ensures a smooth and emulsified dressing that stands out from simple lemon dressings with crumbled feta.

METHOD: MIXING
TIME: PREP TIME: 5 MINUTES / TOTAL TIME: 5 MINUTES
SERVING: 4 PERSON

✓ Mini food processor | ✓ Measuring cups and spoons

INGREDIENTS

- 1/4 cup fresh lemon juice (1 large lemon) (60 ml)
- 1/4 cup extra virgin olive oil (60 ml)
- 1/4 cup crumbled feta (35 g)
- 1 tsp Dijon mustard (5 ml)
- 1/2 tsp salt (3 g)
- 1/2 tsp dried basil (or other herb, optional) (0.5 g)
- 1/4 tsp black pepper (0.5 g)

INSTRUCTIONS

Step 1 |
Combine Ingredients Place the fresh lemon juice (60 ml), extra virgin olive oil (60 ml), crumbled feta (35 g), Dijon mustard (5 ml), salt (3 g), dried basil (0.5 g), and black pepper (0.5 g) into a mini food processor.

Step 2 |
Process Process the ingredients until smooth and creamy. This ensures the feta is fully emulsified into the dressing, giving it a rich and creamy texture.

Step 3 |
Adjust and Serve Taste the vinaigrette and adjust the seasoning if necessary. Serve immediately or refrigerate until ready to use.

NOTES

- **Process, don't stir:** Blending the feta is crucial for a smooth and creamy texture. Stirring will not achieve the same emulsification.
- **Use fresh lemon:** Fresh lemon juice is key to achieving the best flavor. Avoid using bottled lemon juice.
- **Herbs:** Dried basil works well, but oregano or thyme can be used as alternatives. Fresh herbs will have a more pungent flavor and can overpower other ingredients, so use them if you prefer a stronger herbal taste.
- **Amount of juice:** The juice from one large lemon can vary, but this recipe is forgiving. If you're a tablespoon short on lemon juice, it will still work well. If you have extra juice, consider adding more olive oil to balance it.

SPICES & SAUCES

9 TAHINI DRESSING

METHOD — MIXING
TIME — 5 MINUTES
SERVING — 4 PERSON
CALORIES — 120

This creamy Tahini Dressing is a versatile and flavorful addition to any dish. The combination of tahini, garlic, lemon juice, and water creates a smooth and tangy dressing that pairs perfectly with salads, roasted vegetables, or as a dip. Adjust the consistency to your liking for a dressing that's perfect for your needs.

- Whisk
- Mixing bowl
- Measuring cups and spoons
- Garlic press or knife

INGREDIENTS

- 1/3 cup tahini
  (approximately 2.7 fl oz or 80 ml)
- 1 clove garlic, minced
- 3 tbsp lemon juice
- 2 tbsp water, more for desired consistency
- Salt to taste

INSTRUCTIONS

Step 1 | Prepare the ingredients
Mince the garlic (1 clove).

Step 2 | Combine ingredients
In a mixing bowl, whisk together the tahini (2.7 fl oz or 80 ml), minced garlic (1 clove), lemon juice (3 tbsp), and water (2 tbsp).

Step 3 | Adjust consistency
Continue whisking until the mixture is smooth. If the dressing is too thick, gradually add more water until the desired consistency is reached.

Step 4 | Season
Add salt to taste, whisking to incorporate.

NOTES

- For a deeper flavor, you can toast the tahini before mixing.
- Store the dressing in an airtight container in the refrigerator for up to one week.
- Use fresh lemon juice for the best flavor.

VEGETARIAN

Vegetarian

QUINOA STUFFED TOMATOES WITH BASIL AND PINE NUTS, ITALY

INGREDIENTS

- 4 large tomatoes (approx. 2 lbs or 900g)
- 1 cup quinoa (6.3 oz or 180g)
- 2 cups vegetable broth (16 fl oz or 475 ml)
- 1/4 cup pine nuts (1.1 oz or 30g)
- 1/4 cup chopped fresh basil (0.2 oz or 5g)
- 2 tablespoons olive oil (1 fl oz or 30 ml)
- 1/2 cup crumbled feta cheese (2.5 oz or 70g)
- 1/4 teaspoon salt (1.5g)
- 1/4 teaspoon black pepper (0.6g)
- 1 garlic clove, minced (approx. 0.1 oz or 3g)

METHOD OVEN
TIME 40 MINUTE
SERVING 4 PERSON
CALORIES 330

Indulge in the rich flavors of Quinoa Stuffed Tomatoes, where each bite combines creamy quinoa, fresh basil, and crunchy pine nuts in a lush tomato. This dish is a feast for the senses, perfect for a special meal.

- ✓ Medium saucepan
- ✓ Skillet
- ✓ Mixing bowl
- ✓ Baking dish
- ✓ Knife
- ✓ Spoon

INSTRUCTIONS

Step 1 | Preheat the Oven
Preheat your oven to 375°F (190°C).

Step 2 | Prepare the Tomatoes
Slice off the top of each tomato (4 large tomatoes) and scoop out the seeds and pulp to create a hollow shell. Set the tomato shells aside.

Step 3 | Cook the Quinoa
Rinse the quinoa (6.3 oz or 180g) under cold water until the water runs clear. In a medium saucepan, bring the vegetable broth (16 fl oz or 475 ml) to a boil. Add the quinoa, reduce heat to low, cover, and simmer for 15 minutes, or until the liquid is absorbed and the quinoa is tender.

Step 4 | Toast the Pine Nuts
While the quinoa is cooking, toast the pine nuts (1.1 oz or 30g) in a dry skillet over medium heat for 3-4 minutes, shaking the pan occasionally until they are golden and fragrant.

Step 5 | Mix the Filling
Fluff the cooked quinoa with a fork and transfer it to a mixing bowl. To the bowl, add the toasted pine nuts, chopped basil (0.2 oz or 5g), olive oil (1 fl oz or 30 ml), crumbled feta cheese (2.5 oz or 70g), minced garlic (0.1 oz or 3g), salt (1.5g), and pepper (0.6g). Stir the mixture until well combined.

Step 6 | Stuff the Tomatoes
Spoon the quinoa mixture into the hollowed-out tomatoes, pressing gently to pack the filling.

Step 7 | Bake the Tomatoes
Place the stuffed tomatoes in a baking dish and bake in the preheated oven for 10 minutes, or until the tomatoes are heated through and the tops are lightly browned.

Step 8 | Serve
Serve the Quinoa Stuffed Tomatoes warm as a delightful Mediterranean-inspired dinner.

NOTES

- For a vegan option, replace feta with vegan cheese
- Use leftover tomato pulp in soups or sauces
- Personalize the filling with different herbs or veggies for extra flavor and nutrition.

VEGETARIAN

2 LEMON AND FETA GRILLED ASPARAGUS, GREECE

This dish combines the fresh, earthy taste of asparagus with a zesty lemon and feta vinaigrette, offering a side that's both simple and sublime. Grilled to perfection, the asparagus takes on a smoky essence that perfectly complements the tangy dressing.

METHOD — OVEN
TIME — 15 MINUTE
SERVING — 4 PERSON
CALORIES — 93

- ✓ Oven Grill
- ✓ Mixing bowl
- ✓ Tongs
- ✓ Serving platter

INGREDIENTS

- 1 1/2 pounds asparagus, trimmed (24 oz or 680g)
- 1 tablespoon oil (0.5 oz or 15 ml)
- Salt and pepper, to taste
- 1/4 cup lemon and feta dressing (2 oz or 60 ml) (Spices & Sauces Chapter)

INSTRUCTIONS

Step 1 | Prepare the Grill
Prepare your oven grill for medium-high heat.

Step 2 | Season the Asparagus
In a mixing bowl, toss the asparagus spears (24 oz or 680g) with oil (0.5 oz or 15 ml), salt, and pepper until evenly coated.

Step 3 | Grill the Asparagus
Taste the hummus and adjust the seasoning with additional salt, lemon juice, or spices as preferred. Transfer the hummus to a serving bowl, drizzle with extra olive oil, and sprinkle with paprika for garnish. Serve with the pita chips.

Step 3 | Serve
Remove the asparagus from the grill and arrange on a serving platter. Drizzle the grilled asparagus with lemon and feta dressing (2 oz or 60 ml) and serve immediately.

NOTES

- This versatile dish pairs wonderfully with grilled meats or a hearty grain salad, making it a perfect addition to any meal.
- Its vibrant flavors and simple preparation make it a must-try for any asparagus lover.

Vegetarian

3 ROASTED PROVENCAL VEGETABLES WITH HERBED QUINOA, FRANCE

METHOD OVEN | **TIME** 45 MINUTE | **SERVING** 4 PERSON | **CALORIES** 320

Relish in the flavors of the Mediterranean with Roasted Provencal Vegetables paired with light and nutty herbed quinoa. This dish showcases the delightful blend of rustic Provencal vegetables, making it a nutritious and fulfilling meal.

- ✓ Large baking sheet
- ✓ Large bowl
- ✓ Mixing spoon
- ✓ Cutting board
- ✓ Medium saucepan
- ✓ Fork
- ✓ Knife
- ✓ Measuring cups and spoons

INGREDIENTS

— For the Roasted Provencal Vegetables:
- 1 medium zucchini, about (8 oz or 227g)
- 1 medium yellow squash, about (8 oz or 227g)
- 1 red bell pepper, cored and sliced (about 4.2 oz or 119g)
- 1 yellow bell pepper, cored and sliced (about 4.2 oz or 119g)
- 1 small eggplant, cut into 1-inch cubes (about 8 oz or 227g)
- 1 red onion, cut into wedges (about 3.9 oz or 110g)
- 3 tbsp olive oil (1.5 fl oz or 45 ml)
- 1 tsp sea salt (5g)
- 1/2 tsp freshly ground black pepper (2.5g)
- 2 tsp Herbes de Provence
- 1 tbsp fresh thyme leaves

— For the Herbed Quinoa:
- 1 cup quinoa, rinsed (6 oz or 170g)
- 2 cups vegetable broth
- 1 tbsp olive oil (0.5 fl oz or 15 ml)
- 1/4 cup freshly chopped parsley
- 1 tbsp fresh lemon juice
- 1 tbsp lemon zest (about 1 tbsp or 6g)
- 1/2 tsp sea salt (2.5g)

INSTRUCTIONS

Step 1 | Preheat the Oven
Preheat your oven to 425°F (220°C).

Step 2 | Prepare the Vegetables
In a large bowl, toss zucchini, yellow squash, red and yellow bell peppers, eggplant, and red onion with olive oil, sea salt, black pepper, and Herbes de Provence.

Step 3 | Roast the Vegetables
Spread the vegetables in a single layer on a large baking sheet. Roast for 30 minutes or until tender and caramelized, stirring halfway through and adding thyme.

Step 4 | Cook the Quinoa
Simultaneously, in a medium saucepan, combine quinoa and vegetable broth and bring to a boil. Reduce heat, cover, and simmer for 15 minutes until the broth is absorbed. Remove from heat, let stand for 5 minutes, then fluff with a fork.

Step 5 | Prepare the Herbed Quinoa
Stir olive oil, parsley, lemon juice, lemon zest, and sea salt into the quinoa.

Step 5 | Serve
Serve the herbed quinoa topped with roasted vegetables.

NOTES

- Substitute vegetables as desired; tomatoes or green beans are great alternatives.
- If Herbes de Provence is unavailable, mix dried thyme, rosemary, basil, and oregano.

VEGETARIAN

4 BUDDHA BOWL WITH FALAFEL AND TAHINI DRESSING, NORTH AFRICA

INGREDIENTS

— For the Falafel:
- 1 cup dried chickpeas, soaked overnight (7 oz or 200g)
- 1 small onion, quartered
- 2 cloves garlic
- 1/4 cup fresh parsley, chopped
- 1/4 cup fresh cilantro, chopped
- 1 tsp ground cumin
- 1 tsp ground coriander
- 1/2 tsp salt
- 1/4 tsp black pepper
- 1/2 tsp baking soda
- 2 tbsp lemon juice
- Oil for frying

— For the Buddha Bowl:
- 4 cups cooked quinoa or brown rice
- 4 cups mixed greens (spinach, arugula, kale)
- 1 cup cherry tomatoes, halved
- 1 cucumber, diced
- 1 bell pepper, sliced
- 1/2 cup red onion, thinly sliced
- 1/4 cup Kalamata olives, pitted
- 1 avocado, sliced
- Tahini dressing (Sauces & Spices chapter)

METHOD PAN
TIME 50 MINUTES
SERVING 4 PERSON
CALORIES 650

This nutrient-packed Buddha Bowl combines fresh greens, wholesome grains, aromatic falafel, and creamy tahini dressing, offering a harmonious balance of flavor and health. This dish is a vibrant celebration of the Mediterranean diet.

- Food processor
- Frying pan
- Whisk
- Measuring cups and spoons

INSTRUCTIONS

Step 1 | Prepare falafel
In a food processor, blend soaked chickpeas, onion, garlic, parsley, cilantro, cumin, coriander, salt, pepper, baking soda, and lemon juice to a coarse mixture. Form into small patties or balls.

Step 2 | Fry falafel
Heat oil in a frying pan over medium heat. Fry falafel until golden (about 3-4 minutes per side). Drain on paper towels.

Step 3 | Assemble Buddha Bowl
Distribute quinoa or brown rice among four bowls. Top with mixed greens, tomatoes, cucumber, bell pepper, onion, olives, and avocado. Add cooked falafel.

Step 4 | Serve
Drizzle tahini dressing over each bowl before serving.

NOTES

- Choose gluten-free grains if needed
- Bake falafel for a lighter option at 375°F (190°C) for 20-25 minutes.
- Store tahini dressing in the fridge for up to a week for easy meals.
- Add cooked lentils or chickpeas for extra vegan protein.

Vegetarian

5 BAKED RATATOUILLE GRATIN WITH HERBED CRUMBS, FRANCE

Immerse yourself in the flavors of summer with Baked Ratatouille Gratin, featuring a colorful array of vegetables like zucchini, bell peppers, eggplant, and tomatoes. This gratin is crowned with a crispy layer of herbed breadcrumbs, providing a delightful crunch that complements the tender vegetables beneath.

METHOD — OVEN
TIME — 1 HOUR 20 MINUTES
SERVING — 6 PERSON
CALORIES — 210

- 9x13-inch (23x33 cm) baking dish
- Aluminum foil
- Mixing bowl
- Cutting boar
- Knife

INGREDIENTS

- 1 medium eggplant, thinly sliced (about 1 lb or 450g)
- 2 medium zucchinis, thinly sliced (about 1 lb or 450g total)
- 1 large red bell pepper, thinly sliced (about 0.5 lb or 225g)
- 1 large yellow bell pepper, thinly sliced (about 0.5 lb or 225g)
- 4 medium tomatoes, thinly sliced (about 1 lb or 450g total)
- 1/4 cup olive oil (60ml)
- Salt and pepper to taste
- 1 tsp dried thyme
- 1 tsp dried oregano
- 2 cloves garlic, minced
- 1 cup breadcrumbs
- 1/4 cup grated Parmesan cheese
- 2 tbsp fresh parsley, finely chopped
- 1 tbsp unsalted butter, melted

INSTRUCTIONS

Step 1 | Preheat Oven
Preheat oven to 375°F (190°C). Grease a 9x13 inch baking dish with olive oil.

Step 2 | Layer Vegetables
Layer eggplant, zucchini, bell peppers, and tomatoes in the dish, alternating and arranging in a spiral from edge to center.

Step 3 | Season Vegetables
Drizzle vegetables with olive oil (60ml), season with salt, pepper, thyme, and oregano. Cover with foil and bake for 40 minutes.

Step 4 | Prepare Herbed Crumbs
Mix breadcrumbs, Parmesan, parsley, garlic, and melted butter in a bowl.

Step 5 | Add Crumbs and Bake
Remove foil, sprinkle breadcrumb mixture over vegetables, and return to oven, uncovered, for 20 minutes until golden.

Step 5 | Serve
Cool slightly before serving.

NOTES

- Fresh herbs enhance flavor; adjust quantities to preference.
- Prepare ahead for an easy weeknight meal.

Vegetarian

6. ROASTED BUTTERNUT SQUASH WITH CHICKPEAS AND TAHINI DRESSING, TUNISIA

METHOD — OVEN
TIME — 45 MINUTES
SERVING — 4 PERSON
CALORIES — 290

Bask in the flavors of Tunisia with this Roasted Butternut Squash and Chickpeas dish, enhanced with a creamy tahini dressing. This delightful recipe pairs the natural sweetness of butternut squash with the nutty crunch of chickpeas, topped with a tangy tahini sauce for a satisfying meal or an impressive side dish.

- Oven
- Baking sheets
- Whisk
- Large bowl
- Measuring cups and spoons
- Smoll bowl

INGREDIENTS

— For the Butternut Squash:
- 1 large butternut squash, peeled, seeded, and cut into 1-inch cubes (about 2.5 lbs or 1.1 kg)

— For the Chickpeas:
- 1 can chickpeas, drained and rinsed (15 oz or 425g)

— For the Tahini Dressing:
- 1/4 cup tahini
- 2 tablespoons lemon juice
- 1 garlic clove, minced
- 3 tablespoons warm water

— Seasoning:
- 2 tablespoons olive oil
- 1 teaspoon ground cumin
- 1/2 teaspoon smoked paprika

— Garnish (optional):
- Fresh parsley, chopped
- Pomegranate seeds

INSTRUCTIONS

Step 1 | Preheat Oven
Preheat the oven to 425°F (220°C). Toss butternut squash with olive oil, cumin, smoked paprika, salt, and pepper in a large bowl.

Step 2 | Roast Squash
Spread the seasoned squash on a baking sheet in a single layer. Roast for 25-30 minutes until tender and caramelized, stirring halfway.

Step 3 | Roast Chickpeas
Toss chickpeas with a little olive oil and salt in a separate bowl. Spread on another baking sheet and roast for the last 15-20 minutes alongside the squash until crispy.

Step 4 | Prepare Dressing
For the dressing, whisk tahini, lemon juice, minced garlic, and warm water in a small bowl until smooth. Season with salt and adjust consistency with more water if necessary.

Step 5 | Combine and Serve
Combine the roasted squash and chickpeas on a serving platter. Drizzle with tahini dressing and garnish with parsley and pomegranate seeds if using.

NOTES

- Toast the tahini before mixing for a deeper flavor
- Serve over greens for a salad-style meal

Vegetarian

7 IMAMBAYILDI WITH PINE NUTS AND CURRANTS, TURKEY

INGREDIENTS

- 4 medium eggplants (about 2 lbs or 900g)
- 1/4 cup olive oil (60 ml)
- 1 large onion, finely chopped
- 3 cloves garlic, minced
- 1 bell pepper, diced
- 1/2 cup pine nuts (70 g)
- 1/4 cup currants (40 g)
- 2 large tomatoes, finely chopped
- 1 tsp sugar
- 1 tsp ground cinnamon
- 1 tsp ground allspice
- 1/2 tsp ground cloves
- 1/2 tsp ground black pepper
- 1 tsp salt, or to taste
- 1/4 cup chopped fresh parsley (15 g)
- 1 tbsp tomato paste (15 g)
- 1 cup warm water (240 ml)

METHOD OVEN
TIME 1 HOUR 10 MINUTE
SERVING 4 PERSON
CALORIES 310

Experience the rich flavors of Turkey with this aromatic Imambayildi, a classic dish that features eggplants stuffed with a sweet and savory filling of currants, pine nuts, and spices. It's a delightful combination that offers a taste of Turkish cuisine's complexity and charm.

- ✓ Cutting board
- ✓ Chef's knife
- ✓ Large skillet
- ✓ Baking dish
- ✓ Aluminum foil
- ✓ Spoon

INSTRUCTIONS

Step 1 | Preheat Oven and Prepare Eggplants
Preheat the oven to 375°F (190°C). Slice eggplants in half lengthwise, hollow out centers to form boats, leaving 1/2 inch of flesh along the skin. Salt the insides, wait 15 minutes, then rinse and dry.

Step 2 | Sauté Onions and Garlic
Heat half the olive oil in a large skillet over medium heat. Sauté onions and garlic until translucent.

Step 3 | Add Bell Pepper, Pine Nuts, and Currants
Add bell pepper, pine nuts, and currants. Sauté until pine nuts are toasted, about 5 minutes.

Step 4 | Cook Tomatoes and Spices
Incorporate tomatoes, sugar, cinnamon, allspice, cloves, pepper, and salt. Cook for 10 minutes until thickened.

Step 5 | Mix and Adjust Seasoning
Off heat, stir in parsley and tomato paste. Adjust seasoning if needed.

Step 6 | Stuff Eggplants and Bake
Fill eggplant boats with the mixture, place in a baking dish, drizzle with remaining olive oil, and add warm water to the dish. Cover with foil.

Step 7 | Bake
Bake covered for 40 minutes, then uncover and bake for an additional 10 minutes until eggplants are tender and tops are golden.

NOTES

- Imambayildi is excellent hot or at room temperature, and flavors deepen if made ahead.

- Serve with bulgur wheat or rice and a side of plain yogurt for a complete meal

Vegetarian

8 ROASTED CAULIFLOWER WITH TAHINI AND TOASTED PINE NUTS, LEBANON

The dish centers around a beautifully roasted cauliflower head, seasoned to perfection and served with a luscious tahini sauce. The added crunch of toasted pine nuts makes this dish not only a visual treat but also a textural delight. This dish is not just food; it's a statement piece that's bound to impress.

METHOD — OVEN
TIME — 55 MINUTE
SERVING — 4 PERSON
CALORIES — 310

- Oven
- Mixing bowl
- Baking dish
- Whisk
- Small bowl
- Skillet
- Brush

INGREDIENTS

- 1 large head of cauliflower, trimmed and cleaned (about 2-3 lbs or 900g-1.4kg)
- 3 tbsp olive oil (45ml)
- 1 tsp sea salt (5g)
- 1/2 tsp ground black pepper (2g)
- 1/2 tsp smoked paprika (1g)
- 1/4 cup pine nuts (30g)
- 1/2 cup tahini (120ml)
- 2 tbsp lemon juice (30ml)
- 1 clove garlic, minced
- 6 tbsp water (90ml)

INSTRUCTIONS

Step 1 | Preparation
Preheat your oven to 400°F (200°C). Prepare the cauliflower by removing leaves and trimming the stem.

Step 2 | Seasoning
In a small bowl, combine olive oil (3 tbsp), sea salt (1 tsp), black pepper (1/2 tsp), and smoked paprika (1/2 tsp). Brush the cauliflower evenly with this mixture.

Step 3 | Roasting
Place the cauliflower in a baking dish. Roast for approximately 45 minutes, or until golden and tender.

Step 4 | Toasting Pine Nuts
While the cauliflower roasts, toast the pine nuts in a skillet over medium heat until golden, about 3-5 minutes, watching closely to avoid burning.

Step 5 | Tahini Sauce
Whisk together tahini (1/2 cup), lemon juice (2 tbsp), minced garlic, and water (6 tbsp) in a mixing bowl until smooth. Season with salt as needed.

Step 6 | Serving
Once roasted, drizzle the cauliflower with tahini sauce and sprinkle with toasted pine nuts. Serve warm.

NOTES

- Feel free to adjust seasoning amounts based on personal taste preferences.
- If preferred, the cauliflower can be roasted in florets, which may require less cooking time.
- Store any leftover tahini sauce in the fridge and use it as a creamy dressing or dip for other dishes.

BONUS CHAPTER
MOCKTAILS

BONUS CHAPTER. MOCKTAILS

1 BLUEBERRY-ROSEMARY LEMON MOCKTAIL

METHOD
MIXING

TIME
5 MINUTE

SERVING
1 PERSON

CALORIES
76

This blueberry-rosemary lemon mocktail is a winner. Loaded with blueberries and fresh lemon juice with just a touch of fresh rosemary, this effervescent mocktail is light and refreshing. The true beauty of mocktails is they offer an easy, tasty, make-ahead option for dinner parties and family gatherings. A kid-friendly alternative to water, they can be low in sugar as well.

- ✓ Cocktail shaker
- ✓ Muddler
- ✓ Drinking glass
- ✓ Spoon
- ✓ Strainer

INGREDIENTS

- 10 fresh blueberries, plus additional for garnish (approx. 0.5 oz or 15g)
- 1 rosemary stem, stripped
  (approx. 1 tsp or 0.5g)
- 1 tablespoon agave
  (approx. 0.5 fl oz or 15ml)
- 1 ounce freshly squeezed lemon juice
  (approx. 2 tbsp or 30ml)
- 6 ounces sparkling mineral water
  (approx. 180ml)
- Rosemary sprig, for garnish (optional)

INSTRUCTIONS

Step 1 | Muddle Ingredients
Using a cocktail shaker, add the blueberries (0.5 oz or 15g), stripped rosemary leaves (0.5g), and agave (0.5 fl oz or 15ml). Muddle for 30 seconds to release the flavors.

Step 2 | Mix and Strain
Add the freshly squeezed lemon juice (2 tbsp or 30ml) to the shaker and stir. Strain the mixture into your preferred drinking glass.

Step 3 | Add Ice and Sparkling Water
Fill the glass with a good amount of crushed ice. Pour in the sparkling mineral water (180ml) and give it a gentle stir.

Step 4 | Garnish and Serve
Garnish with additional fresh blueberries and a rosemary sprig if desired. Serve immediately and enjoy this refreshing mocktail.

NOTES

- This mocktail can be prepared ahead of time by making the blueberry-rosemary syrup and storing it in the refrigerator for up to 3 days.

- For a sweeter mocktail, increase the amount of agave or substitute with honey or simple syrup.

BONUS CHAPTER. MOCKTAILS

2 GRAPEFRUIT-THYME SODA MOCKTAIL

INGREDIENTS

- 3 thyme sprigs, divided
  (approx. 3 tsp or 1.5g)
- 1 1/2 teaspoons agave
  (approx. 0.25 fl oz or 7.5ml)
- 2 ounces freshly squeezed red grapefruit juice (approx. 4 tbsp or 60ml)
- 1 ounce freshly squeezed orange juice (approx. 2 tbsp or 30ml)
- 1 ounce freshly squeezed lime juice (approx. 2 tbsp or 30ml)
- Sparkling mineral water

METHOD MIXING
TIME 5 MINUTES
SERVING 1 PERSON
CALORIES 72

This grapefruit-thyme soda is light, fruity, and effervescent. With subtle herbal notes and just a touch of sweetness, it's a keeper no matter what your drink constitution may be.

- ✓ Cocktail shaker
- ✓ Muddler
- ✓ Strainer
- ✓ Drinking glass
- ✓ Spoon

INSTRUCTIONS

Step 1 | Muddle Ingredients
In a cocktail shaker, add the thyme leaves from one sprig (1 tsp or 0.5g) and the agave (0.25 fl oz or 7.5ml). Use a muddler to muddle the thyme leaves slightly to release their flavor.

Step 2 | Add Juices and Ice
Add the freshly squeezed red grapefruit juice (4 tbsp or 60ml), orange juice (2 tbsp or 30ml), lime juice (2 tbsp or 30ml), and a generous handful of ice to the shaker.

Step 3 | Shake and Strain
Shake vigorously for 30 seconds to combine and chill the ingredients. Strain the mixture into a cocktail glass.

Step 4 | Add Ice and Sparkling Water
Add some crushed ice to the glass. Top with sparkling mineral water to taste.

Step 5 | Garnish and Serve
Garnish with the additional fresh thyme sprigs. Serve immediately and enjoy this refreshing mocktail.

NOTES

- This mocktail can be prepared ahead of time by making the grapefruit-thyme syrup and storing it in the refrigerator for up to 3 days.

- For a sweeter mocktail, increase the amount of agave or substitute with honey or simple syrup.

3 BLACKBERRY AND CINNAMON SHRUB

INGREDIENTS

- 250g (9 oz) granulated sugar
- 250ml (9 fl oz) water
- 450-500g (1-1lb 2oz) blackberries
- 1/4-1/2 teaspoon ground cinnamon
- 200ml (7 fl oz) raw apple cider vinegar
- Sparkling water or apple juice and sparkling water, to serve

METHOD MIXING
TIME 20 MINUTES + 24-48h resting time
SERVING 8 PERSON

Blackberry and Cinnamon Shrub is perfect for turning your freshly picked blackberries into a flavorful beverage, this shrub integrates the deep, rich taste of cooked blackberries with the warm spice of cinnamon, creating a harmonious and refreshing drink. Enjoy it as a mocktail base or mix with sparkling water for a refreshing treat.

- ✓ Saucepan
- ✓ Fine sieve
- ✓ Bowl
- ✓ Funnel
- ✓ Sterilized bottle

INSTRUCTIONS

Step 1 | Dissolve Sugar
Put the sugar (250g or 9 oz) in a saucepan and add the measured water (250ml or 9 fl oz). Heat over a low heat, stirring occasionally, until the sugar has completely dissolved.

Step 2 | Cook Blackberries
Bring the mixture to a boil and add the blackberries (450-500g or 1-1lb 2oz) and cinnamon (1/4-1/2 teaspoon), then simmer for 10-12 minutes until the blackberries are soft.

Step 3 | Macerate
Take off the heat and leave to macerate for about 15 minutes.

Step 4 | Strain Mixture
Tip the contents of the pan into a fine sieve over a bowl and leave to strain, then press down gently on the berries to extract their juice.

Step 5 | Add Vinegar
Stir the vinegar (200ml or 7 fl oz) into the liquid.

Step 6 | Bottle and Refrigerate
Pour the mixture through a funnel into a sterilized bottle, seal, and leave in the refrigerator for at least 24-48 hours. It will keep for 2-3 weeks in the refrigerator.

Step 7 | Serve
To serve, dilute 4:1 or 5:1 with sparkling water or half apple juice and half sparkling water.

NOTES

- For best flavor, use high-quality apple cider vinegar.
- The shrub can be stored in the refrigerator for up to 2-3 weeks.
- Adjust the amount of cinnamon according to your taste preference.

BONUS CHAPTER. MOCKTAILS

4 FROZEN STRAWBERRY AND WATERMELON MARGARITA

Strawberry and watermelon is a great combination even without the tequila of a classic Margarita, though you could add a shot or two of alcohol-free vodka if you like. Obviously, it's best made in summer when both strawberries and watermelon are ripe – the perfect drink to sit and sip in the garden. You don't have to add salt to the rim of your glass – it's equally delicious without.

METHOD
MIXING

TIME
10 MINUTE

SERVING
2 PERSON

- ✓ Blender
- ✓ Knife
- ✓ Cutting board
- ✓ Juicer
- ✓ Saucer
- ✓ Glass

INGREDIENTS

- 1 fresh lime, halved
- Sea salt flakes (optional)
- Handful of ice cubes
- 175g (6 oz) strawberries, hulled and halved, plus an extra slice to garnish
- 175g (6 oz) watermelon, peeled, deseeded, and cut into chunks
- Sugar syrup, to taste (optional)
- Basil, to garnish

INSTRUCTIONS

Step 1 | Prepare Lime and Rim the Glass
Juice half the lime. To salt the rim of your glass, wipe the cut surface of the other lime half around the rim of each glass, then dip into a saucer of sea salt flakes.

Step 2 | Crush Ice
Crush the ice cubes in a powerful blender, or wrap them in a clean tea towel and smash with a rolling pin if your blender isn't powerful enough.

Step 3 | Blend Ingredients
Add the strawberries (175g or 6 oz) and watermelon chunks (175g or 6 oz) and 1 tablespoon of the lime juice to the crushed ice in the blender and whizz until you get a frozen slush.

Step 4 | Adjust Sweetness and Serve
Check for sweetness, adding extra lime juice or sugar syrup to taste if needed, then pour into a chilled martini glass. Garnish with a basil leaf and a slice of strawberry.

NOTES

- For an extra refreshing twist, chill the fruits before blending.

- This mocktail is perfect for summer gatherings and can be made in larger quantities.

- If you prefer a more traditional margarita, you can add a shot of tequila to the blend.

5 MULLED "WINE"

METHOD PAN | **TIME** 35 MINUTE | **SERVING** 6-8 PERSON | **CALORIES** 320

Although alcohol-free wine doesn't quite cut it for wine drinkers, it makes a decent mulled wine. The key is to add elderberry juice to give the drink body, but it is quite bitter, so add sugar to taste.

- ✓ Saucepan
- ✓ Small knife
- ✓ Cutting board
- ✓ Fine sieve
- ✓ Bowl
- ✓ Sterilized bottle

INGREDIENTS

- 8 cloves
- 2 unwaxed oranges
- 75cl bottle alcohol-free red wine
- 330ml (11 fl oz) elderberry juice
- 125g (4½ oz) soft brown sugar
- 1 cinnamon stick
- Orange oil or orange bitters (optional)

INSTRUCTIONS

Step 1 | Prepare Ingredient
Stick the cloves into the rind of one orange. Pour the alcohol-free wine and elderberry juice into a small-medium saucepan. Add 125g (4½ oz) sugar, the cinnamon stick, and 2-3 drops of orange oil or a shake of orange bitters.

Step 2 | Simmer and Infuse
Bring slowly up to simmering point over a low heat without letting it boil. Take off the heat and leave for 30 minutes to infuse.

Step 3 | Serve
To serve, reheat the mulled "wine". Slice the remaining orange and place a slice into six to eight small cups or heatproof glasses. Pour over the hot mulled "wine" and serve.

NOTES

- Add more or less sugar to adjust the sweetness.
- This drink can be stored in the refrigerator and reheated gently before serving.
- Serve with a cinnamon stick in each glass for added flavor.

MEDITERRANEAN DIET PYRAMID

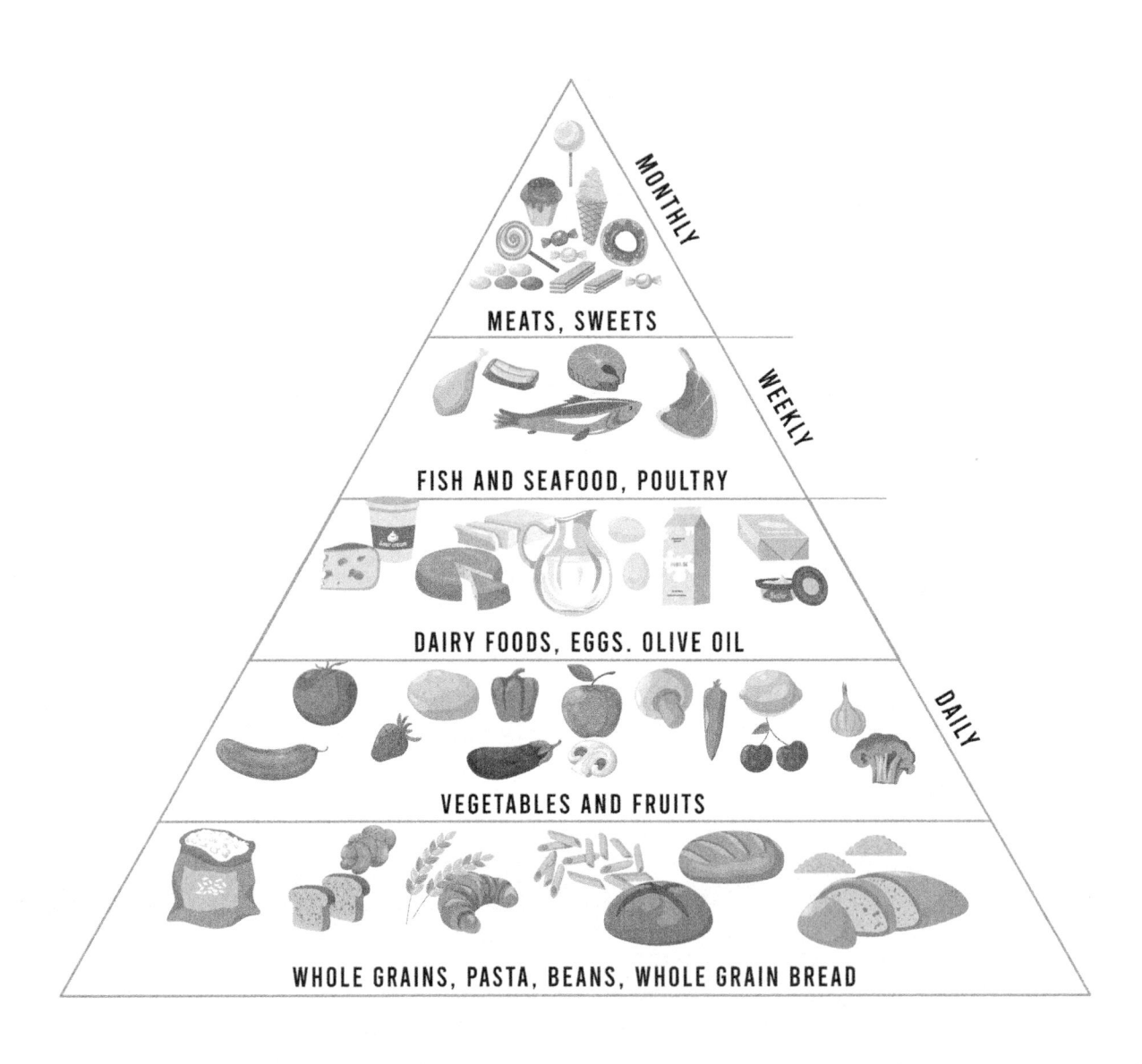

MONTHLY — MEATS, SWEETS

WEEKLY — FISH AND SEAFOOD, POULTRY

DAILY
- DAIRY FOODS, EGGS, OLIVE OIL
- VEGETABLES AND FRUITS
- WHOLE GRAINS, PASTA, BEANS, WHOLE GRAIN BREAD

CONVERSION TABLE

VOLUME EQUIVALENTS (LIQUID)

STANDARD	US STANDARD (OUNCES)	METRIC (APPROXIMATE)
2 tablespoons	1 fl. oz.	30 mL
¼ cup	2 fl. oz.	60 mL
½ cup	4 fl. oz.	120 mL
1 cup	8 fl. oz.	240 mL
1½ cups	12 fl. oz.	355 mL
2 cups or 1 pint	16 fl. oz.	475 mL
4 cups or 1 quart	32 fl. oz.	1 L
1 gallon	128 fl. oz.	4 L

VOLUME EQUIVALENTS (DRY)

STANDARD	METRIC (APPROXIMATE)
⅛ teaspoon	0.5 mL
¼ teaspoon	1 mL
½ teaspoon	2 mL
¾ teaspoon	4 mL
1 teaspoon	5 mL
1 tablespoon	15 mL
¼ cup	59 mL
⅓ cup	79 mL
½ cup	118 mL
⅔ cup	156 mL
¾ cup	177 mL
1 cup	235 mL
2 cups or 1 pint	475 mL
3 cups	700 mL
4 cups or 1 quart	1 L

WEIGHT EQUIVALENTS

STANDARD	METRIC (APPROXIMATE)
½ ounce	15 g
1 ounce	30 g
2 ounces	60 g
4 ounces	115 g
8 ounces	225 g
12 ounces	340 g
16 ounces or 1 pound	455 g

OVEN TEMPERATURE

FAHRENHEIT	CELSIUS (C) (APPROXIMATE)
250°	120°
300°	150°
325°	165°
350°	180°
375°	190°
400°	200°
425°	220°
450°	230°

WEEKLY MEAL PLAN WEEK 1

FROM: / /   TO: / /

	BREAKFAST	LUNCH	DINNER
MON	Overnight Oats with Greek Yogurt and Fresh Figs (BREAKFAST RECIPES, pg. 9)	White Bean Salad with Tomatoes and Parsley (PULSES RECIPES, pg. 50)	Shrimp Scampi with Lemon-Garlic Butter Sauce (FISH & SEAFOOD RECIPES, pg. 18)
TUE	Egg White Scramble with Asparagus and Sun-Dried Tomatoes (BREAKFAST RECIPES, pg. 7)	Chicken Gyros With Pita Bread & Tzatziki Sauce, Greece (POULTRY RECIPES, pg. 45)	Broccoli and Sausage Penne (PASTA RECIPE, pg. 37)
WED	Roasted Red Pepper and Feta Frittata (BREAKFAST RECIPES, pg. 8)	Quinoa Tabbouleh with Fresh Herbs and Lemon (SALADS & MEZZES RECIPES, pg. 60)	Mackerel with Harissa and Preserved Lemons (FISH & SEAFOOD RECIPES, pg.15)
TUE	Savory Oatmeal with Spinach and Poached Eggs (BREAKFAST RECIPES, pg. 11)	Tuna Melt Stuffed Bell Peppers (FISH & SEAFOOD RECIPES, pg. 19)	Zucchini Lasagna with Turkey and Pesto (PASTA RECIPE, pg. 38)
FRI	Ricotta and Berry Stuffed French Toast (BREAKFAST RECIPES, pg. 12)	Pasta with Roasted Tomatoes and Almond Pesto (PASTA RECIPE, pg.33)	Ribollita with Kale and Crispy Pancetta (PULSES RECIPES, pg. 51)
SAT	Couscous Breakfast Bowl with Dates and Almonds (BREAKFAST RECIPES, pg. 13)	Green Olive Salad with Lemon and Parsley (SALADS & MEZZES RECIPES, pg. 61)	Roasted Beef Tenderloin (MEAT RECIPES, pg. 23)
SUN	Buddha Bowl with Falafel and Tahini Dressing (VEGETARIAN RECIPES, pg. 87)	Roasted Cauliflower with Tahini and Toasted Pine Nuts, Lebanon (VEGETARIAN RECIPES, pg. 91)	Baked Ratatouille Gratin with Herbed Crumbs, France (VEGETARIAN RECIPES, pg. 88

WEEKLY SHOPPING LIST   WEEK 1

FROM: / /   TO: / /

Vegetables

- Brussels sprouts: 453g
- Red onion: 270g
- Cherry tomatoes: 300g
- Asparagus tips: 67g
- Sun-dried tomatoes: 113g
- Spinach: 117g
- Garlic: 150 g
- Onions: 713g
- Green onions: 43g
- Bell pepper: 170g
- Zucchini: 680g
- Romanesco broccoli: 300g
- Kale: 300g
- Mixed greens
- Cucumber: 150g
- Avocado: 120g
- Lentils: 200g

Fruit

- Fresh figs: 160g
- Mixed berries: 150g
- Lemon: 60ml juice, 1 zest
- Dates: 88g
- Fresh mint leaves: for garnish

Grains, Nuts, and Seeds

- Rolled oats: 180g
- Couscous: 180g
- Quinoa: 300g
- Almonds: 30g
- Dried Chickpeas: 200g

Canned and Packaged Goods

- Gnocchi: 453g
- Penne pasta: 340 g
- Chicken broth: 475ml
- White beans: 425g
- Unsweetened almond milk: 240 ml
- Preserved Lemons: 2 pcs
- Eggs: 12pcs
- Roasted Red Peppers: 150 g
- Kalamata Olives: 1 can
- Tahini: 100 ml
- Baking Soda

Bread and Toast

- Pita bread: 4
- Crusty bread: for serving

Meat & Seafood

- Meat & Seafood
- Shrimp: 454g
- Ground turkey: 454g
- Mackerel fillets: 680g
- Italian sausage: 454g
- Beef tenderloin: 1360g

Dairy

- Greek yogurt: 297g
- Feta cheese: 100g
- Ricotta cheese: 250g
- Parmesan cheese: 90g
- Mozzarella cheese: 240g
- Whole milk: 120ml
- Heavy Cream: 240 ml

Herbs & Spices (chek your stock first)

- Fresh basil: 20g
- Fresh dill: 10g
- Fresh mint: 15g
- Fresh parsley: 30g
- Fresh cilantro: 20g
- Fresh Thyme
- Ground cumin: 10g
- Ground coriander: 10g
- Dried Oregano
- Saffron threads
- Olive oil
- Smoked Paprika: 20g
- Cayenne pepper: 10 g
- Salt and pepper: to taste
- Granulated sugar
- Maple syrup
- Powdered sugar
- Thyme: 10g
- Ground Cinamon
- White wine vinegar
- Italian seasoning
- Corn starch
- Dry white wine
- Unsalted butter
- Tahini 1/2 cup
- Dried currants 40g
- Ground Cloves
- Ground allspice
- Red Wine Vinegar

WEEKLY MEAL PLAN WEEK 2

FROM: / / TO: / /

	BREAKFAST	LUNCH	DINNER
MON	Overnight Oats with Greek Yogurt and Fresh Figs (BREAKFAST RECIPES, p. 9)	Tuna Melt Stuffed Bell Peppers (FISH & SEAFOOD RECIPES, p. 19)	Zucchini Lasagna with Turkey and Pesto (PASTA RECIPE, p. 38)
TUE	Egg White Scramble with Asparagus and Sun-Dried Tomatoes (BREAKFAST RECIPES, p. 7)	Tuna and Potato Salad, Spain (SALADS & MEZZES RECIPES, p. 63)	Imambayildi with Pine Nuts and Currants (VEGETARIAN RECIPES, p. 90)
WED	Couscous Breakfast Bowl with Dates and Almonds (BREAKFAST RECIPES, p. 13)	Red Lentil and Quinoa with Cumin (PULSES RECIPES, p. 54)	Baked Beans with Tomatoes and Dill (PULSES RECIPES, p. 48)
TUE	Ricotta and Berry Stuffed French Toast (BREAKFAST RECIPES, p. 12)	Beet and Yogurt Salad (SALADS & MEZZES RECIPES, p. 62)	Casserole Fish with Onions and Tomatoes (FISH & SEAFOOD RECIPES, p. 21)
FRI	Spanish Chorizo Shakshuka with Piquillo Peppers (BREAKFAST RECIPES, p. 10)	Lentils with Rice and Caramelized Onions (PULSES RECIPES, p.49)	Chicken with Rice (POULTRY RECIPES, p. 46)
SAT	Savory Oatmeal with Spinach and Poached Eggs (BREAKFAST RECIPES, p.11)	Grilled Vegetable Gazpacho with Fresh Basil (SALADS & MEZZES RECIPES, p.72)	Baked Ratatouille Gratin with Herbed Crumbs (VEGETARIAN RECIPES, p. 88)
SUN	Chilled Avocado and Cucumber Soup with Mint and Yogurt (SOUP RECIPES, p. 71)	Buddha Bowl with Falafel and Tahini Dressing (VEGETARIAN RECIPES, p. 87)	Roasted Carrot Soup with Ginger and Orange (SOUP RECIPES, p. 68

WEEKLY SHOPPING LIST — WEEK 2

FROM: / /   TO: / /

Vegetables

- Bell peppers: 2 pieces
- Zucchini: 3 pieces
- Asparagus: 1 bunch
- Sun-Dried Tomatoes: 100g
- Beet: 1 piece
- Onions: 4 pieces
- Tomatoes: 6 pieces
- Spinach: 200g
- Cucumber: 1 large
- Carrots: 2 pieces
- Eggplants: 4 pieces

Fruit

- Fresh figs: 160g
- Dates: 88g
- Fresh berries: 150g

Grains, Nuts, and Seeds

- Rolled oats: 180g
- Quinoa: 170g
- Almonds: 30g
- Dried Chickpeas: 200g
- Pine nuts: 70g

Canned and Packaged Goods, Pasta

- Canned chickpeas: 425g
- Canned diced tomatoes: 400g
- Tomato paste: 30g
- Crushed tomatoes: 1 can
- Piquillo Peppers: 1 Jar

Bread and Toast

- Pita breads: 4 pieces

Meat & Seafood

- Ground turkey: 900g
- Solid Yellowfin Tuna in Extra Virgin Olive Oil: 255g
- White fish fillets: 907g
- Chorizo: 113g
- Chicken: 500g

Dairy

- Eggs: 12 large
- Greek yogurt: 500g
- Ricotta cheese: 250g

Herbs & Spices (chek your stock first)

- Fresh basil: 20g
- Fresh dill: 10g
- Fresh mint: 15g
- Fresh parsley: 30g
- Fresh cilantro: 20g
- Fresh Thyme
- Ground cumin: 10g
- Ground coriander: 10g
- Dried Oregano
- Saffron threads
- Olive oil
- Smoked Paprika: 20g
- Cayenne pepper: 10 g
- Salt and pepper: to taste
- Granulated sugar
- Maple syrup
- Powdered sugar
- Thyme: 10g
- Ground Cinamon
- White wine vinegar
- Italian seasoning
- Corn starch
- Dry white wine
- Unsalted butter
- Tahini 1/2 cup
- Dried currants 40g
- Ground Cloves
- Ground allspice
- Red Wine Vinegar

WEEKLY MEAL PLAN   WEEK 3

FROM: / /   TO: / /

	BREAKFAST	LUNCH	DINNER
MON	Spanish Chorizo Shakshuka with Piquillo Peppers (BREAKFAST RECIPES, p. 10)	Tuna and Potato Salad, Spain (SALADS & MEZZES RECIPES, p. 63)	Tuna Melt Stuffed Bell Peppers (FISH & SEAFOOD RECIPES, p. 19)
TUE	Egg White Scramble with Asparagus and Sun-Dried Tomatoes (BREAKFAST RECIPES, p. 7)	Beet and Yogurt Salad (SALADS & MEZZES RECIPES, p. 62)	Zucchini Lasagna with Turkey and Pesto (PASTA RECIPE, p. 38
WED	Overnight Oats with Greek Yogurt and Fresh Figs (BREAKFAST RECIPES, p. 9)	Lentils with Rice and Caramelized Onions (PULSES RECIPES, p. 49)	Chicken with Rice (POULTRY RECIPES, p. 46)
TUE	Couscous Breakfast Bowl with Dates and Almonds (BREAKFAST RECIPES, p. 13)	Red Lentil and Quinoa with Cumin (PULSES RECIPES, p. 54)	Baked Beans with Tomatoes and Dill (PULSES RECIPES, p. 48)
FRI	Ricotta and Berry Stuffed French Toast (BREAKFAST RECIPES, p. 12)	Buddha Bowl with Falafel and Tahini Dressing (VEGETARIAN RECIPES, p. 87)	Imambayildi with Pine Nuts and Currants (VEGETARIAN RECIPES, p. 90)
SAT	Savory Oatmeal with Spinach and Poached Eggs (BREAKFAST RECIPES, p. 11)	Grilled Vegetable Gazpacho with Fresh Basil (SALADS & MEZZES RECIPES, p. 72)	Baked Ratatouille Gratin with Herbed Crumbs (VEGETARIAN RECIPES, p. 88)
SUN	Chilled Avocado and Cucumber Soup with Mint and Yogurt (SOUP RECIPES, p.71)	Buddha Bowl with Falafel and Tahini Dressing (VEGETARIAN RECIPES, p. 87)	Roasted Carrot Soup with Ginger and Orange (SOUP RECIPES, p 68.)

WEEKLY SHOPPING LIST — WEEK 3

FROM: / /   TO: / /

Vegetables

- Bell peppers: 4 pieces
- Zucchini: 2 pieces
- Asparagus: 67g
- Sun-dried tomatoes: 100g
- Beet: 1 piece
- Onions: 6 pieces
- Tomatoes: 6 pieces
- Spinach: 200g
- Cucumber: 1 large
- Carrots: 2 pieces
- Eggplants: 4 pieces
- Avocados: 2 pieces
- Cherry tomatoes: 150g
- Red onions: 1 piece
- Fresh figs: 160g
- Green olives: 150g
- Red bell pepper: 1 piece

Fruit

- Bananas: 2
- Dates: 88g
- Fresh berries: 150g

Grains, Nuts, and Seeds

- Rolled oats: 180g
- Quinoa: 170g
- Almonds: 30g
- Dried Chickpeas: 200g
- Pine nuts: 70g

Canned and Packaged Goods, Pasta

- Canned chickpeas: 425g
- Canned diced tomatoes: 400g
- Tomato paste: 30g
- Crushed tomatoes: 1 can
- Piquillo Peppers: 1 Jar

Bread and Toast

- Pita breads: 4 pieces

Meat & Seafood

- Ground turkey: 900g
- Solid Yellowfin Tuna in Extra Virgin Olive Oil: 255g
- White fish fillets: 907g
- Chorizo: 113g
- Chicken: 500g

Dairy & Eggs

- Eggs: 12 large
- Greek yogurt: 500g
- Ricotta cheese: 250g

Herbs & Spices (chek your stock first)

- Fresh basil: 20g
- Fresh dill: 10g
- Fresh mint: 15g
- Fresh parsley: 30g
- Fresh cilantro: 20g
- Fresh Thyme
- Ground cumin: 10g
- Ground coriander: 10g
- Dried Oregano
- Saffron threads
- Olive oil
- Smoked Paprika: 20g
- Cayenne pepper: 10 g
- Salt and pepper: to taste
- Granulated sugar
- Maple syrup
- Powdered sugar
- Thyme: 10g
- Ground Cinamon
- White wine vinegar
- Italian seasoning
- Corn starch
- Dry white wine
- Unsalted butter
- Tahini 1/2 cup
- Dried currants 40g
- Ground Cloves
- Ground allspice
- Red Wine Vinegar

WEEKLY MEAL PLAN WEEK 4

FROM: / / TO: / /

	BREAKFAST	LUNCH	DINNER
MON	Overnight Oats with Greek Yogurt and Fresh Figs (BREAKFAST RECIPES, p. 9)	Tuna and Potato Salad, Spain (SALADS & MEZZES RECIPES, p. 63)	Casserole Fish with Onions and Tomatoes (FISH & SEAFOOD RECIPES, p. 21)
TUE	Egg White Scramble with Asparagus and Sun-Dried Tomatoes (BREAKFAST RECIPES, p. 7)	Quinoa Tabbouleh with Fresh Herbs (SALADS & MEZZES RECIPES, p. 60	Sun-Dried Tomato Chicken (POULTRY RECIPES, p. 41)
WED	Ricotta and Berry Stuffed French Toast (BREAKFAST RECIPES, p. 12)	Culdo verde with Chorizo and Kale (SOUP RECIPES, p. 67	Beef Tenderloin Roast (MEAT RECIPES, p. 24)
TUE	Couscous Breakfast Bowl with Dates and Almonds (BREAKFAST RECIPES, p. 13)	Red Lentil and Quinoa with Cumin (PULSES RECIPES, p. 54)	Lemon and Thyme Roasted Sea Bass (FISH & SEAFOOD RECIPES, p. 17)
FRI	Spanish Chorizo Shakshuka with Piquillo Peppers (BREAKFAST RECIPES, p. 10)	White Bean Salad with Tomatoes and Parsley (PULSES RECIPES, p. 50)	Ricotta and Saffron Dumplings (PASTA RECIPE, p. 36)
SAT	Savory Oatmeal with Spinach and Poached Eggs (BREAKFAST RECIPES, p. 11)	Grilled Vegetable Gazpacho with Fresh Basil (SOUP RECIPES, p. 72)	Artichoke and Olive Pasta with Lemon and Garlic (PASTA RECIPE, p. 32)
SUN	Roasted Red Pepper and Feta Frittata (BREAKFAST RECIPES, p. 8)	Roasted Butternut Squash with Chickpeas and Tahini Dressing (VEGETARIAN RECIPES, p. 89)	Imambayildi with Pine Nuts and Currants (VEGETARIAN RECIPES, p. 90)

WEEKLY SHOPPING LIST   WEEK 4

FROM: / /   TO: / /

Vegetables

- Asparagus: 100g
- Bell peppers: 400g
- Cherry tomatoes: 100g
- Cucumber: 100g
- Eggplants: 1.3kg
- Fresh figs: 100g (4)
- Garlic: 100g
- Green olives: 50g
- Onions: 700g
- Potatoes: 700g
- Red onions: 100g
- Spinach: 100g
- Tomatoes: 700g
- Zucchini: 1
- Kale: 300g
- Butternut squash: 1 large
- Carrots: 100g
- Celery: 100g

Fruit

- Bananas: 2
- Dates: 88g
- Fresh berries: 150g
- Lemons: 5

Grains, Nuts, and Seeds

- Couscous: 180g
- Pine nuts: 50g
- Quinoa: 200g
- Semolina flour: 480g
- Almonds: 50g
- Rolled Oats: 180g
- Tahini: 50g
- Medjool dates: 4 pcs

Canned and Packaged Goods, Pasta

- Canned white beans: 200g
- Canned chickpeas: 1 can
- Canned diced tomatoes: 400g
- Tomato paste: 30g
- Pasta: 200g (350)
- Honey: 50g
- Sun-Dried Tomatoes: 30g 80
- Vanilla extract
- Piquillo peppers 1 jar
- Roasted red peppers 150 g
- Kalamata Olives 50 g
- Canned artichoke hearts: 1 can

Meat & Seafood

- Chicken breasts: 680g
- White Fish Fillet 900g
- Tuna: 255g
- Sea bass: 700g
- Beef tenderloin: 1360g
- Chorizo sausage: 400g

Herbs & Spices (chek your stock first)

- Fresh basil: 20g
- Fresh dill: 10g
- Fresh mint: 15g
- Fresh parsley: 30g
- Fresh cilantro: 20g
- Fresh Thyme
- Ground cumin: 10g
- Ground coriander: 10g
- Dried Oregano
- Saffron threads
- Olive oil
- Smoked Paprika: 20g
- Cayenne pepper: 10 g
- Salt and pepper: to taste
- Granulated sugar
- Maple syrup
- Powdered sugar
- Thyme: 10g
- Ground Cinamon
- White wine vinegar
- Italian seasoning
- Corn starch
- Dry white wine
- Unsalted butter
- Tahini 1/2 cup
- Dried currants 40g
- Ground Cloves
- Ground allspice
- Red Wine Vinegar

Bread and Toast

- Brioche: 8 slices

Dairy & Eggs

- Eggs: 12 large
- Feta cheese: 50g
- Greek yogurt: 400g
- Ricotta cheese: 550g
- Pecorino cheese: 60g
- Whole grain bread: 100g
- Butter: 50g
- Milk: 1l
- Unsweetened almond milk: 240ml

INDEX PAGE

BREAKFAST

EGG WHITE SCRAMBLE WITH ASPARAGUS AND SUN-DRIED TOMATOES, ITALY	7
ROASTED RED PEPPER AND FETA FRITTATA, CYPRUS	8
OVERNIGHT OATS WITH GREEK YOGURT AND FRESH FIGS, GREECE	9
SPANISH CHORIZO SHAKSHUKA WITH PIQUILLO PEPPERS, SPAIN	10
SAVORY OATMEAL WITH SPINACH AND POACHED EGGS, FRANCE	11
RICOTTA AND BERRY STUFFED FRENCH TOAST, FRANCE	12
COUSCOUS BREAKFAST BOWL WITH DATES AND ALMONDS, ALGERIA	13

FISH & SEAFOOD

MACKEREL WITH HARISSA AND PRESERVED LEMONS, NORTH AFRICA	15
UMBRIAN BAKED TROUT WITH TOMATOES AND OLIVES, ITALY	16
LEMON AND THYME ROASTED SEA BASS, ITALY	17
SHRIMP SCAMPI WITH LEMON-GARLIC BUTTER SAUCE, ITALY	18
TUNA MELT STUFFED BELL PEPPERS, CROATIA	19
TUNA STEAK WITH OPTIONAL GARLIC HERB SAUCE, ITALY	20
CASSEROLE FISH WITH ONIONS AND TOMATOES, GREECE	21

MEAT

ROASTED LAMB AND POTATOES, CRETE	23
BEEF TENDERLOIN ROAST RECIPE, LEBANON	24
GRILLED LAMB CHOPS WITH ROSEMARY, CORSICA	25
OSSO BUCO WITH GREMOLATA AND SAFFRON RISOTTO, ITALY	26
BEEF PICCATA, ITALY	27
LAMB MEATBALLS WITH TZATZIKI AND POMEGRANATE GLAZE, GREECE	28
RABBIT STEW WITH VEGETABLES AND WHITE WINE, IBIZA	29
LAMB STEW WITH HERBS AND WHITE BEANS, CORSICA	30

PASTA

ARTICHOKE AND OLIVE PASTA WITH LEMON AND GARLIC, ITALY	32
PASTA WITH ROASTED TOMATOES AND ALMOND PESTO, ITALY	33
COUSCOUS WITH ROASTED VEGETABLES AND LEMON DRESSING, ISRAEL	34
SPAGHETTI WITH FRESH SARDINES AND WILD FENNEL, SICILY	35
RICOTTA AND SAFFRON DUMPLINGS (MALLOREDDUS), SARDINIA	36

BROCCOLI AND SAUSAGE PENNE (PENNE ALLA ROMANESCA), ITALY	37
ZUCCHINI LASAGNA WITH TURKEY AND PESTO, ITALY	38

POULTRY

SHEET-PAN CHICKEN THIGHS WITH BRUSSELS SPROUTS & GNOCCHI, ITALY	40
SUN-DRIED TOMATO CHICKEN, ITALY	41
CHICKEN SOUVLAKI WITH OREGANO AND GARLIC, GREECE	42
CHICKEN STIFADO WITH ONIONS AND CINNAMON, GREECE	43
ROASTED CHICKEN WITH PRUNES AND CINNAMON, TURKEY	44
CHICKEN GYROS WITH PITA BREAD & TZATZIKI SAUCE, GREECE	45
CHICKEN WITH RICE, SPAIN	46

PULSES

BAKED BEANS WITH TOMATOES AND DILL, GREECE	48
LENTILS WITH RICE AND CARAMELIZED ONIONS (MUJADDARA), CYPRUS	49
WHITE BEAN SALAD WITH TOMATOES AND PARSLEY (PIYAZ), TURKEY	50
RIBOLLITA WITH KALE AND CRISPY PANCETTA, ITALY	51
SAUERKRAUT AND BEAN STEW (JOTA), SLOVENIA	52
STUFFED EGGPLANT WITH LENTILS, WALNUTS, AND POMEGRANATE GLAZE, LEBANON	53
RED LENTIL AND QUINOA WITH CUMIN, NORTH AFRICA	54

SALADS & MEZZES

BULGUR WHEAT SALAD WITH TOMATOES AND CUCUMBERS (KISIR), TURKEY	56
BAKED FETA WITH HONEY AND SESAME SEEDS, ALBANIA	57
ROMAN ARTICHOKES (CARCIOFI ALLA ROMANA), ITALY	58
ROASTED PEPPERS WITH GARLIC AND PARSLEY, ITALY	59
QUINOA TABBOULEH WITH FRESH HERBS AND LEMON, SYRIA	60
GREEN OLIVE SALAD WITH LEMON AND PARSLEY, TURKEY	61
BEET AND YOGURT SALAD (PANCAR SALATASI), TURKEY	62
TUNA AND POTATO SALAD, SPAIN	63

SOUP

EGGPLANT AND CHICKPEA STEW WITH CUMIN, SYRIA	65
MINESTRA SOUP WITH BEANS AND GREENS, CORSICA	66
CALDO VERDE WITH CHORIZO AND KALE, PORTUGAL	67
ROASTED CARROT SOUP WITH GINGER AND ORANGE, SPAIN	68
LENTIL AND PUMPKIN STEW, SICILY	69

ANDALUSIAN CHILLED ALMOND SOUP (AJO BLANCO), SPAIN	70
CHILLED AVOCADO AND CUCUMBER SOUP WITH MINT AND YOGURT, SPAIN	71
GRILLED VEGETABLE GAZPACHO WITH FRESH BASIL, SPAIN	72

SPICES & SAUCES

CHERMOULA SAUCE, NORTH AFRICA	74
OLIVE AND CAPERS TAPENADE, MALLORCA	75
TZATZIKI WITH CUCUMBER AND DILL, GREECE	76
POMEGRANATE GLAZE	77
ANATOLIAN ROASTED RED PEPPER HUMMUS WITH PITA CHIPS, TURKEY	78
TAHINI DRESSING, CYPRUS	79
PESTO GENOVESE WITH WALNUT AND MINT, ITALY	80
LEMON FETA VINAIGRETTE	81
TAHINI DRESSING	82

VEGETARIAN

QUINOA STUFFED TOMATOES WITH BASIL AND PINE NUTS, ITALY	84
LEMON AND FETA GRILLED ASPARAGUS, GREECE	85
ROASTED PROVENCAL VEGETABLES WITH HERBED QUINOA, FRANCE	86
BUDDHA BOWL WITH FALAFEL AND TAHINI DRESSING, NORTH AFRICA	87
BAKED RATATOUILLE GRATIN WITH HERBED CRUMBS, FRANCE	88
ROASTED BUTTERNUT SQUASH WITH CHICKPEAS AND TAHINI DRESSING, TUNISIA	89
IMAMBAYILDI WITH PINE NUTS AND CURRANTS, TURKEY	90
ROASTED CAULIFLOWER WITH TAHINI AND TOASTED PINE NUTS, LEBANON	91

BONUS CHAPTER. MOCKTAILS

BLUEBERRY-ROSEMARY LEMON MOCKTAIL	93
GRAPEFRUIT-THYME SODA MOCKTAIL	94
BLACKBERRY AND CINNAMON SHRUB	95
FROZEN STRAWBERRY AND WATERMELON MARGARITA	96
MULLED "WINE"	97

MEDITERRANEAN DIET PYRAMID — 98

CONVERSION TABLE — 99

MEAL PLAN. SHOPPING LIST — 100

Copyright © 2024 by Lavinia Baresi. All rights reserved.

No part of this publication may be reproduced, distributed, or transmitted in any form or by any means, including photocopying, recording, or other electronic or mechanical methods, without the prior written permission of the publisher, except in the case of brief quotations embodied in critical reviews and certain other non-commercial uses permitted by copyright law.

Disclaimer of Liability: The publisher and the author do not guarantee the accuracy, completeness, or usefulness of the information presented in this book and will not be liable for any errors or omissions in this information nor for the availability of this information. The publisher and the author will not be liable for any losses, injuries, or damages from the display or use of this information. This book is not intended to be a replacement for professional medical advice and should not be interpreted as such. Any application of the techniques, ideas, and suggestions in this book is at the reader's sole discretion and risk.

Printed in Great Britain
by Amazon